A HUNDRED YEARS EATING

James P. Johnston

A HUNDRED YEARS EATING

Food, Drink and the Daily Diet
in Britain since the
late Nineteenth Century

Gill and Macmillan
McGill-Queen's University Press

First published in 1977

Gill and Macmillan Ltd
15/17 Eden Quay
Dublin 1
McGill–Queen's University Press
1020 Pine Avenue West
Montreal H3A 1A2
and internationally through
association with the
Macmillan Publishers Group

7171 0747 7 (Gill and Macmillan)

0 7735 0306 4 (McGill–Queen's)

Legal Deposit 3rd Quarter 1977
Bibliothèque Nationale du Québec

Acknowledgment is due to Miss D. E. Collins
for permission to quote from
'The Song Against Grocers' from
The Collected Poems of G. K. Chesterton (Methuen)

Printed in England by
Bristol Typesetting Co. Ltd Barton Manor St Philips Bristol

To my Mother and Father

Contents

List of Illustrations

Preface

Food is absolutely vital to man's existence : without it he cannot live. It is therefore somewhat surprising to find that in the past historians have devoted only scant attention to this basic necessity of life. The purely physiological aspect of food consumption has undoubtedly led many to believe that the study of what men eat should be left to nutritionists, biologists and chemists. In recent years, however, the study of diet has begun to occupy the attention of a growing number of social historians, who have come to recognise the significance of food, not only in terms of the physical needs of men, but also as an essential element in economic and social life. Recent 'socio-dietary' historical studies have shown that we can learn much not only about individuals but also about society as a whole by examining what men eat. More important, however, from the historian's point of view is the fact that these studies have also revealed a close historical relationship between the course of economic and social change and patterns of food consumption. As a result, they have opened the door to an entirely new field of historical research.

This book represents an attempt to do no more than illustrate the nature of the association between economic and social and dietary change over the past one hundred or so years in relation to Britain. It does not pretend to cover new ground; indeed, the author is only too aware of his debt to the work of other writers, as many as possible of whom have been listed in the bibliography. However, it is hoped that this book will serve for layman and historian alike as a useful introduction to this interesting yet much neglected area of study. A work of this sort is necessarily subject to limitations both of time and space. For that reason, references have been used only to cite the sources of quotations and to suggest additional reading on particular subjects. A short note on statistical sources can be found at the end of the book.

I am indebted to Professor William Ashworth, who read the complete typescript and whose comments and suggestions enabled me to correct some of my more glaring errors, to Dr Ken Brown, at whose suggestion the decision to undertake the work was made and who made several useful comments on the final draft, and to my wife, Dolores, whose encouragement and support were invaluable.

J. P. Johnston

I

An Historical Contrast: The Economy, Society and Diet of Britain since 1900

[i]

THE DEATH of Queen Victoria and the accession of King Edward VII to the throne of England in 1901 in many ways marked the end of an era in British history. As that age to which Victoria had lent her name drew to a close—an age which had seen Britain grow in power and assurance under the driving force of her industrial pre-eminence—the 'Workshop of the World' was already beginning to abdicate its premier position in the international economy, in the face of growing competition from newly emerging industrial nations. Nevertheless, the process of industrialisation had brought in its wake many sweeping changes in the nature of the economy and society of Britain. During the course of the nineteenth century huge urban conglomerations, fostered by the spread of factory industry, had produced a new breed of people— the urban working class, whose numbers were swelling relentlessly—while economic prosperity had also produced a new class of industrialists, financiers and bankers, who were already, by the end of the nineteenth century, laying challenge to the long-established hegemony of the landed aristocracy.

However, despite these developments, at the beginning of Edward's reign Britain remained a highly stratified society, and despite some diminution in economic and political power, it was still the landed aristocracy who set the social standards assiduously aped by that amorphous group collectively termed the middle class. The middle class ranged at one extreme from the top industrialists and financiers, many of whom eventually merged into the aristocracy, down through the professions to, at the lower end of the scale, small shopkeepers and clerks, a substantial proportion of whom earned less than skilled manual workers yet were accorded a higher social standing than them. Within it, incomes varied considerably, ranging from £160 per year at the lower levels to £2,000 and over among those at the top of the professions. Even at the bottom of the scale, however, earnings were generally sufficient to provide a reasonably comfortable standard of living.

Below the middle class came that 80 per cent of the population who made up the working class. Within this group, however, there was no more homogeneity than in the classes above. Indeed, in many ways the working class was a microcosm of British society as a whole at the time, possessing its own scales of income and social status. At the top of the labour tree stood that 10–15 per cent of the working class who formed the labour 'aristocracy' or elite. These were skilled craftsmen who could earn as much as 50s per week. In general, they were better housed, better fed and better educated than the vast majority of working men. Below them came the semi-skilled, typically a machine operator. They represented the largest single group of workers at this time, with wages varying between 25s and 35s per week. Next came the unskilled, who included amongst their ranks general labourers, navvies, domestic servants and agricultural labourers. Wages in this group varied considerably, ranging from 25s per week downwards. In general, of all adult male workers, agricultural labourers received the lowest wages. Below the unskilled came the unemployables, the misfits, the tramps and the destitute, described by William Booth, the founder of the Salvation Army, as 'the submerged tenth'. All of these groups were differentiated not only by income but also by attitudes and behaviour. In the words of one contemporary observer,

> There is as much variety of opinion and of ambition among the working classes in England as among those above them. They include as many sections and schools, with differences as wide and divisions as deep, as the upper classes, or as that complex multitude known as the middle classes. It is therefore impossible to label them with any single epithet or any one characteristic, unless, indeed, it should be said that they are law-abiding.[1]

Despite these differences, all had one thing in common : in manners, style of life, dress, speech, and interests, they were clearly distinguishable from the middle and upper classes, who regarded them alike as inferior to themselves.

In purely economic terms, however, the lot of the working class as a whole had improved considerably since the mid-nineteenth century. Between 1850 and 1900 average real wages had risen by some 80 per cent, and sections of the working class appeared to be making impressive strides towards comfort and prosperity. Nevertheless, despite this improvement, and despite the belief, fostered by it, that all classes alike were at last sharing in the fruits of industrialisation, the overall distribution of income in Britain was only marginally more equitable in 1900 than it had been fifty years earlier. By the early years of the present century British society was still characterised by gross inequalities in income, and particularly by the yawning gap which separated the rich from the poor. Leo Chiozza Money highlighted this division in his book *Riches and Poverty* (1905). According to his estimate, in 1904 some 5 million people in Britain took half the national income for themselves, while the other 39 million, making up the labouring class, had to make do with the other half. At the very top of the income scale came that $2\frac{1}{2}$ per cent of the population who between them owned over two-thirds of the total wealth of the country.

The results of this inequality were to be seen in the everyday life of countless working-class families as they struggled continuously against social and material degradation. As late as 1901, despite the advances made during the preceding thirty years, poverty and destitution were still outstanding features of life in Britain. The sombre disclosures of Charles Booth and B. Seebohm Rowntree concerning the extent of poverty in London and York came as an unpleasant shock to many contemporaries. The picture these and later investigators presented was not one of a well-fed and comfortable working class, but rather of an impoverished mass stunted and debilitated by a hundred years of industrial life. Employing a stringent measure of a subsistence level based on the smallest amount of food necessary to maintain 'mere physical efficiency', Rowntree concluded in his *Poverty: A Study in Town Life* (1901) that nearly 28 per cent of the population of York were living in a state of poverty. A few years earlier, on the basis of a similar definition of poverty, Charles Booth, in his pioneering study *Life and Labour of the People* (1889–91), had estimated that over 30 per cent of the population of London were living below the breadline. Subsequent investigations revealed a no less disturbing picture in other areas of the country. For example, one survey of the four towns, Northampton, Warrington, Stanley and Reading, revealed that some 16 per cent of the working class in these towns were living in a state of primary poverty, while it was discovered that in Reading over 45 per cent of those under the age of fourteen were living at near-starvation level. The plight of working-class children was also highlighted in the *Report of the Interdepartmental Committee on Physical Deterioration* (1904). According to this report, a third of all children at the time were undernourished to the extent that they actually went without food for a great part of the time. Widespread malnutrition resulted in stunted growth among many working-class children. Rickets and other deficiency diseases were common and it was discovered that twelve-year-old boys attending private schools were on average five inches taller than those attending council schools. Throughout the country the poverty and hunger of a large section of the working masses contrasted painfully with the opulence of the rich. Jack London, an American visitor to Britain at the time, dramatised in the following words the picture which confronted him :

> From all the land rises the hunger wail, from Ghetto and countryside, from prison and casual ward, from asylum and workhouse—the cry of the people who have not enough to eat. Millions of people, men, women, children, little babes, the blind, the deaf, the halt, the sick, vagabonds and toilers, prisoners and paupers, the people of Ireland, England, Scotland, Wales, who have not enough to eat.[2]

Today, some seventy years after the disturbing revelations of these early social investigators, British society bears little resemblance to the picture just described. Technological and economic change, along with the pressures of two world wars, have radically transformed the pattern of life in Britain. The so-called 'affluent society' in which we live today has been the product of a great rise in the standard of living of the majority of the population, particularly since 1945. Improved living standards have, in their turn, brought about significant changes in social attitudes and cultural activities. In the political sphere, the emergence of new ideas and the implementation of new policies aimed at improving the lot of the underprivileged have virtually eradicated poverty of the kind described by Booth and Rowntree at the turn of the century. Pockets of distress and deprivation do, it is true, remain, but few people now actually go hungry.

Over the past seventy years the occupational structure of Britain has also changed dramatically. The tertiary or service sector of the economy has expanded rapidly, while the industrial sector and the industrial workforce have declined, in relative terms, both in size and importance. Between 1911 and 1966 the number of white-collar occupations in Britain grew by an estimated 176 per cent, while over the same period the increase in the number of manual occupations was only in the region of 5 per cent. This, of course, has resulted in a considerable swelling in the ranks of the middle class, who now represent over 40 per cent of the total population. Perhaps more significant is the fact that the yawning gap which divided the working class from those above at the turn of the century has been considerably narrowed. Indeed, in terms of income, aspirations and lifestyle, a large section of the working class is now almost indistinguishable from those of moderate income traditionally regarded as middle class simply by virtue of their employment in non-manual labour.

However, to say that there has been a levelling in overall life-styles is not to say that class differences have disappeared—Britain is still one of the most class-ridden countries in the world—only that the dichotomy between rich and poor which characterised the Britain of old has been noticeably reduced. The possession of consumer goods provides a good indication of this trend. For example, in 1972 it was estimated that 96 per cent of the population owned a television, 81 per cent owned a re-frigerator, 73 per cent a washing machine and 43 per cent a motor-car. More significantly, even in the lowest income group composed of unskilled manual labourers, ownership of these goods stood at 94 per cent, 56 per cent, 60 per cent and 16 per cent respectively.

One of the most outstanding features of this levelling process can be seen in the dramatic change which has taken place in British eating habits over the past seventy years. Indeed, there could be no more striking illustration of the transformation of the economy and society of Britain during the course of the twentieth century than the contrast between the diet of the British people at the turn of the century and that of today.

[ii]

The inequalities in income which characterised the Edwardian era were poignantly reflected in the contrasting diets of the upper and lower classes at that time. Indeed, nowhere was the extent of the chasm dividing the working class from those above so apparent as on the dinner table. Solely in terms of the quantity of food consumed, the gulf was alarmingly wide. One survey of domestic budgets, carried out in 1902, estimated that upper-class families consumed, on average, about three times as much meat as working-class households each year, four times as much milk and three times as much butter. Among the aristocracy those gargantuan feasts which had characterised the Victorian age continued to display all the affluence expected of a prosperous ruling class. King Edward himself, who was noted for his epicurean tastes, set the standards in *haute cuisine* avidly imitated by those who could afford the luxury of a first-class French chef and a large retinue of servants. Breakfast at Sandringham usually consisted of haddock or bloater, poached eggs, bacon, chicken and woodcock (when, of course, in season). Having managed to wade through a twelve-course luncheon and a dinner of the same proportions, the King, before going to bed, might indulge himself with a late-night snack of, perhaps, plovers' eggs, ptarmigan and salmon.

Slightly lower down the social scale, dinner parties continued to provide the middle-class family with the opportunity to display not only the culinary *savoir faire* of the mistress of the house, but also the economic well-being of the household. These affairs, which by the end of the nineteenth century usually consisted of between eight and ten courses, would vary in their regularity according to the means of the family. By this time the traditional method of service, *à la française*, whereby several courses were placed before the diners at the same time, had already been replaced in most homes by the more recent method, *à la russe*, by which each course would be served consecutively by waiters. A dinner served in the latter fashion might have begun with an *hors d'oeuvre*, followed, in order, by soup (usually two kinds, one clear and one thick), fish (again usually two kinds, one boiled and one fried), an entree, a joint, a roast, vegetables, a hot sweet, a cold sweet, and finally coffee and liqueurs.

Dining out was also popular among the middle and upper classes, and as with the dinner party, the regularity and quality of meals eaten outside the home varied with income. There was, in fact, a scale of restaurants to match the various levels on the income scale. At the very top came the best London establishments such as the Ritz and the Carlton Hotel, over which presided such distinguished French chefs as César Ritz and the great Escoffier. In the plush surroundings of these high-class restaurants the rich would savour the delights of the finest in French *haute cuisine*. Take, for example, the following menu which was served at the Carlton Hotel on 6 July 1903, on the occasion of the visit of the President of the French Republic to London:

Caviar frais — Melon cantaloup
Potage béarnais
Consommé aux nids d'hirondelle
Filet de truite au chambertin
Poularde aux perles du Périgord
Nouilles au beurre noisette
Mignonette d'agneau Clarence
Petits pois à la française
Suprême d'écrevisse
Neige au champagne
Caille escortée d'ortolans
Coeur de laitue
Asperges crême d'Isigny
Pêche Alexandra
Parfait aux trois couleurs
Mignardises[3]

Of course, a meal at the Carlton or the Ritz would have been above the means of the majority of the middle class. For those further down the social scale who enjoyed dining out, a number of restaurants such as the Trocadero or the Hotel Russell provided good food in pleasant surroundings and at reasonable prices; and even lower down the scale, a fairly decent meal could be had in Soho for as little as three or four shillings.

However, social history is not simply the history of high society, and at a more mundane level the Edwardian bourgoisie did not always eat in such lavish style. The normal everyday diet of the middle class would certainly have varied with the income of the family, but a fairly typical household, living on about £1,000 per year, would, on average, manage to consume three good meals a day. Each meal would usually consist of four courses, and a typical dinner might have included, for example, pea and ham soup for starters, followed by braised sweetbreads, roast fillet of beef with cauliflower and mashed potatoes, then, perhaps, a savoury of sardines on toast, followed by cheese and dessert.

It has often been suggested that the food of the middle class at this time lacked variety and excitement. For example, one writer has recently claimed that 'Edwardian recipe books give the impression that middle- and upper-class meals tended to consist of elaborately decorated constructions for the purpose of entertaining and sufficient but gastronomically dull food for purely domestic purposes.'[4] This may have been the case thirty years earlier, but it could hardly be said of the middle-class diet of Edwardian times. During the latter decades of the nineteenth century a number of developments had taken place which, by the early years of the present century, were already having a profound effect on the diet of all classes alike in Britain. Important advances in the field of technology and, more specifically, in the field of transport, along with the opening up of vast new areas of food production in America and Australia, had helped effect a virtual revolution in the food supplies of Britain. From the 1870s onwards massive quantities of cheap imported foodstuffs were flooding onto the British market. These included not only basic foods such as meat, grain, fish, etc., but also a wide range of delicacies, including a large number of tinned products, which added colour and variety to the diet of the middle class. In fact, the principal beneficiaries of these developments were those people at the lower end of the middle class, who were increasingly able to satisfy their demands for products formerly reserved for those further up the income scale.

The effects of these developments were not, however, solely confined to the middle class, for they also had important consequences for the diet of the labouring masses. Around the middle of the nineteenth century the working class in Britain survived on a diet largely composed of bread, bacon, cheese, potatoes and tea. However, as observed earlier, from the 1850s the fortunes of this section of the population took a decided turn for the better, and with average real earnings steadily increasing, many working-class families enjoyed a rising standard of living, at least until the early years of the present century when prices began to rise and the increase in real wages came to a halt. Despite this latter set-back, it has been estimated that income per head rose by as much as £30 per year between 1851 and 1911. This figure, of course, is an average and, as will become clear later, obscures vast differ-ences in the fortunes of various sections of the working class. What is certain, however, is that over this sixty-year period money wages doubled and the cost of living fell considerably for a large section of the working population. The biggest increases in real income came after 1874, when imports in large quantities brought the prices of a number of commodities tumbling down. Among the most important items affected by price falls were wheat, sugar, cheese, bacon, ham and lard, all of which figured prominently in the diet of the working class. Reductions in the prices of all these products helped reduce the cost of the working man's food bill by some 30 per cent.

The widespread adoption of refrigeration, dating from the 1880s, gave further impetus to the downward trend of prices as shipments of frozen pork and lamb from America and Australia began to bring meat onto the tables of numerous working-class families at prices which they could now begin to afford. By the latter decades of the nineteenth century deep-sea trawlers were coming into greater use, bringing abundant supplies of cheap Icelandic cod into Britain. One of the principal outlets for this product came to be that traditional working-class institution, the fish and chip shop. Having spread quickly during the 1880s and 1890s from what has claimed to be the place of its origin in Oldham, it had already become an important factor in the diet of the poor by the turn of the century.

With the prices of basic foods declining during the last quarter of the nineteenth century, consumption of a number of other commodities rapidly increased as families with some money to spare began to satisfy their demands for fruit, vegetables and dairy produce among other things. It was estimated, for example, that in 1902 ordinary wage-earners were already consuming each year an average of 15 lb of butter, 10 lb of cheese and $8\frac{1}{2}$ gallons of milk. Technological advances and the adoption of cheaper, mass-production methods of food processing gave added weight to the downward pressure on prices. The consumption of former luxuries such as cocoa and jam rapidly increased, while that of tea and sugar doubled during the last fifty years of the nineteenth century. A number of completely new products appeared on the market. Several of these, such as margarine and condensed milk, quickly entered the diet of the working class, serving as cheap substitutes for fresh produce. In the field of food distribution, the arrival of the multiple retail store, along with the growth of the Co-operative Wholesale Society and Co-operative retail societies, helped reduce prices even further, in addition to improving the quality and increasing the availability of a wide range of products both new and old.

However, although it is certain that abundant supplies of a number of foodstuffs were becoming increasingly available at relatively low prices, thereby reducing the cost of the average weekly food bill, it is equally certain that for a large section of the working class the resulting rise in the value of real wages simply meant that the demand for basic foods could be more easily satisfied. For that 30 per cent of the population who were living close to, and often below, the level of subsistence, the food supply revolution of the late nineteenth century meant more in theory than in practice. Where former luxuries were coming to figure in the diet of working-class families, in many instances they did so in such small quantities that any nutritional benefits which might have been gained from a more varied diet must have been lost, more often than not, in the subdivision, or 'doling out', of the available supply among the several members of the family. In any case, with prices turning upwards once more during the early years of the present century, many of the gains made during the previous thirty years were quickly eroded. The most convincing evidence of the continuing monotony of the diet of a large section of the working class at the turn of the century can be found in a brief perusal of some family budgets of the period. Rowntree, for example, in his survey of York, provides us with a number of detailed accounts of the income and expenditure of working-class families in that town.

A fairly typical example from this survey is that of a labourer, married with three young daughters, and earning an average of 25s per week.[5] Set out in Table 1 is a list of all the food purchases made by this family during the week ending 22 February 1901.

Table 1

Food purchased during the week ending 22 February 1901

Friday	¾ stone flour, 1s 1d; 2 lb sugar, 3d; ¼ lb tea, 4½d; yeast, 1d; 1 lb raisins, 5d; 1 lb sweets, 3d; ¼ lb baking powder, 5d; ½ lb lard, 2½d; ½ lb butter, 7d; 1 lb 2 oz bacon, 7d; 2 lb bread, 2½d; ½ lb beef steak, 6d.
Saturday	3 lb beef, 3s; milk (per week), 1s; ½ lb fish, 3d.
Tuesday	½ lb liver, 2d; 1 lb onions, 1½d; 1 lb cheese, 8d; 2 lb treacle, 3d.
Wednesday	1 lb brawn, 6d.
Thursday	¼ lb butter, 3½d; 1 lb bacon, 6d.

This list provides a useful indication of the prices of various food-stuffs at the turn of the century, but more importantly, it also shows clearly just how narrow a range of items could be afforded on such a limited budget. This family was spending over half its weekly income on food, yet, with the exception of some onions and raisins, no fruit or vegetables appear on the list, no biscuits or cakes, no jam or margarine, and no condiments of any description, nor is there any evidence of the use of canned foods of any kind. Bread, meat and bacon predominate in the list, making for the monotonous menu of meals shown in Table 2.

Apart from being monotonous, the diet of this family was, of course, grossly deficient in protein, and it is important to bear this in mind, since this household was described by Rowntree as being very careful in its expenditure, with the husband indulging in 'no unnecessary luxuries'. This was certainly not the case in a large number of working-class families where the father might often be a heavy drinker or the mother might simply be a bad housekeeper. For whatever reason, a family's expenditure on food could be, and often was, reduced to the level of the poorest households, in which over two-thirds of the weekly income had to be spent on food and in which fresh meat was rarely eaten more than once a week. Indeed, more often than not many of these

Table 2

Menu of meals provided during week ending 22 February 1901

	Breakfast	Dinner*	Tea	Supper
Friday	Bacon Bread Tea	Stew	Steak Bread Tea	
Saturday	Bacon Bread Tea	Beef Potatoes	Hotcake Butter Tea	Fish Potatoes
Sunday	Bacon Bread Tea	Beef Potatoes Yorkshire pudding	Tea Bread Butter Sweet cake	Cold meat Bread
Monday	Bread Butter Treacle Tea	Cold beef Potatoes Rice pudding	Toast Butter Tea	
Tuesday	Cocoa Bread Butter	Liver Onions Potatoes Suet pudding	Bread Butter Treacle Tea	Bread Cheese
Wednesday	Dripping Toast Tea	Soup	Meat Bread Tea	
Thursday	Bread Butter Tea	Bacon Bread Tea	Bread Butter Tea	

* Unlike the middle and upper classes, for whom it represented the evening meal, among the working class dinner was generally eaten at midday. However, many lower-middle class families also dined at midday—a habit which constituted one of the criteria for their lower-middle class status and which distinguished them from those further up the social scale.

families were obliged to exist on a diet of bread and margarine
with cheese and sometimes kippers and bacon.

Even where the house was well kept the family diet might be
much worse than a weekly menu of meals such as that shown
above might suggest. For if it is remembered that all the meals
listed above were produced from the list of purchases presented
earlier, then it is apparent that the food must have been appor-
tioned, particularly in the case of a large family, in minute shares.
To complicate the matter further, working-class eating habits
ensured that not everyone had an equal share of what food was
available. In many households it was the practice for the father
always to have his meal first, for he was the principal wage-
earner and had to be kept healthy at all costs. He, in turn, would
usually be followed by any other wage-earning members of the
family, and finally by the children. Robert Roberts in his book
The Classic Slum recounted the typical dining procedure in his
native Salford around this time:

> Father ate his fill first, 'to keep his strength up', though natur-
> ally the cost of protein limited his intake of meats. He dined
> in single state or perhaps with his wife. Wage-earning youth
> might take the next sitting, while the younger end watched,
> anxious that any titbit should not have disappeared before
> their turn came. Sometimes all the children ate together: a
> basic ration of, say, two slices (and no more) of bread and
> margarine being doled out.[6]

In the course of this doling-out process, Roberts recalled, small
girls usually came off worst of all, since it was somehow felt that
they needed less food than boys. However, it is clear that all of
the children suffered badly from this practice and, indeed, as
already observed, child undernourishment was one of the most
repugnant features of the time. The gravity of the situation was
captured in the following words of a contemporary giving evidence before the committee investigating the extent of physical
deterioration in the country:

> Want of food, irregularity and unsuitability of food, taken
> together are the determining cause of degeneracy in children.
> The breakfasts that these children get are nominally bread and
> tea, if they get it at all. There is bread and margarine for lunch,

and the dinner is normally nothing but what a copper can purchase at the local fried fish shops, where the most inferior kinds of fish such as skate are fried in unwholesome, reeking cottonseed oil. They frequently supplement this with rotten fruit, which they collect beneath barrows.[7]

This same person also drew attention to what was surely one of the most serious problems of the time as regards infant feeding: the shortage of fresh milk in towns. This was one of the main causes of the underfeeding of babies. Condensed milk, the cheapest varieties of which were made from skimmed milk and could be bought in penny tins, was a popular but poor substitute, possessing few of the nutritive powers of fresh milk. However, all too often even this was not available, and babies were fed instead on table scraps of bread, tea and boiled potatoes. Baby foods, as we know them today, were, it is true, on the market before the outbreak of war in 1914, but their high cost kept them out of reach of the vast majority of working-class families. It was estimated in 1909 that partly as a result of this underfeeding, nearly 110 out of every 1,000 children died before reaching the age of one.

In the countryside the plight of the rural labouring class was even worse than that of its counterpart in the cities. Here the chasm dividing the upper from the lower classes was even more blatant, and the romantic image of a happy and well-nourished peasantry bears little relation to fact. On the contrary, while His Lordship and Her Ladyship up at the country mansion might have sat down to a mighty breakfast of porridge, kidney omelet, baked eggs, fried and grilled ham, potted game, veal cake, stewed prunes and cream, scones, rolls, toast, bread, butter, marmalade, jam, tea, coffee, cream and milk, the majority of rural labourers would often have had little more than tea, bread and butter to sustain them through a hard morning's work.

The appalling conditions under which Britain's agricultural labourers toiled were revealed by Seebohm Rowntree in his book *How the Labourer Lives* (1912). Although the average earnings of the rural labourer were around 18s per week, including 'perks' such as cheap milk, rent of cottage, harvest money, etc., the majority had to live on much less than this. Furthermore, by this time, contrary to the common belief, food was no cheaper in the countryside than in the towns. Indeed, during the latter decades of the nineteenth century the flood of cheap imported foodstuffs into the urban centres of Britain and the rise of multiple retailing with its emphasis on price competition led to a steady reduction in the cost of living for the urban labourer which was not shared by his rural counterpart, who remained dependent for most of his food on the monopolistic village shop. For example, Rowntree cited a family of seven living in Oxfordshire with a weekly income of only 12s, which was by no means exceptional.[8] A list of the expenditure of this family on food for a typical week in 1912 (see Table 3) is revealing in itself. These paltry purchases were supple-

Table 3

Expenditure on food during typical week in November 1912

	s	d
40 lb bread	4	7
¼ stone flour		5½
½ lb potted butter		6
9½ pints milk	1	2
⅔ lb pearl barley		2
5 lb sugar		10
1 lb rice		2
¼ lb suet		1½
2 lb bones		2
½ lb bacon		4
½ lb tea		6
Total	9	0

mented by what could be produced on the small allotment which the family rented for 14s 4d per annum. For this typical week in November 1912 the consumption of home produce was estimated to be: 27 lb potatoes, 3 lb turnips, 2 lb carrots, 5 lb greens and ½ lb onions. Together, these provisions enabled the formulation of the menu of meals for the week shown in Table 4. In addition, Rowntree tells us that the baby of the family was fed on pearl barley and milk (about one pint a day) and that the father sometimes took with him to work a piece of bread and butter or dry bread to eat between breakfast and dinner.

Table 4

Menu of meals provided during typical week in November 1912

	Breakfast	Dinner	Tea	Supper
Friday	Tea Bread Butter	Suet pudding baked in oven Potatoes Greens	Tea Bread (*butter if* *any left*)	Tea Bread
Saturday	Tea Bread Dripping (*from bones* *or meat*)	Bread Dripping or sugar Tea	Tea Bread (*butter if* *any left*)	Tea Bread
Sunday	Tea Bread Butter	Bacon Potatoes Suet pudding Greens	Tea Bread Butter	Tea Bread Butter (*for two*)
Monday	Tea Bread Butter	Bacon (*for man*) Potatoes Bread	Tea Bread Butter	Tea Bread Butter
Tuesday	Tea Bread Butter	Bacon Potatoes Bread	Tea Bread Butter	Tea Bread
Wednesday	Tea Bread Butter	Soup made of bones, rice, carrots, turnips; suet dumplings, onions, potatoes	Tea Bread Butter	Tea Bread Soup
Thursday	Tea Bread Butter	Boiled rice with bones, vegetables	Tea Bread Butter	Tea Bread Soup

Once again, as in the example cited earlier, the subdivision of the available food between the several members of the family meant that the quantities actually consumed by each person would in all likelihood be very small, except in the case of bread, which was the mainstay of the family's diet. The food supply revolution of the late nineteenth century had clearly made little impact on this household, for not only was the diet devoid of variety, but it was also grossly deficient in protein and other nutritional necessities.

Undoubtedly, therefore, at the beginning of the twentieth century the diet of the British people vividly reflected the rigid class divisions in society itself. Just as the working class was so clearly distinguished from the middle and upper classes, so too was the food of the working man vastly different from that of the professional or business gentleman. The most important element in the maintenance of this differential was income, and as long as the yawning gap separating the working class from those above remained, this was bound to be the case. Monotony and nutritional deficiency in his diet would continue to be the lot of the working man so long as he remained at, or close to, the margin of subsistence. It is true, as observed earlier, that the developments of the late nineteenth century, which were revolutionising the food supply of Britain, had already made an important impact on the diet of the working class as the prices of basic commodities declined and the range of foodstuffs becoming more readily available steadily increased. However, by the early years of the present century the rise in working-class living standards was already being halted by rising prices. By this time the most significant benefits of the revolution in Britain's food supplies were accruing to the better-off sections of the working class and, more especially, to the lower middle class. Despite some improvement in their diet, the majority of the working class, including that 30 per cent who were living in a state of poverty, were destined to wait some time before reaping the full benefits of the advances of the late nineteenth century.

In retrospect, it is possible to draw impressive comparisons with the past. The great economic and social changes which have taken place since the turn of the century have radically transformed the nature of British society. Rising living standards among the mass of the population have considerably narrowed the income gap between classes and have helped to swell the ranks of the middle class. One of the most interesting offshoots of this latter development has been the growing importance of middle-class standards in the diet of the British people as a whole. Nowadays it is as much a rarity to see an upper-class, Victorian-sized meal as it is to see such monotonous and nutritionally deficient diets as those described earlier. In the course of the levelling of living standards since the Edwardian era, the diet of the working class has improved beyond all recognition. In quantitative terms, an indication of the effect of growing affluence among working-class families is the fact that food now forms a much smaller proportion of total expenditure than it did at the turn of the century. Even in the poorest households today it rarely accounts for more than 25 per cent of total expenditure, in contrast to the levels of 60 per cent and more suggested by Rowntree and others seventy years ago.

But not only has the average diet improved; the food itself has also changed considerably. Today we eat much less of the traditional, basic foods such as bread, meat and fish, and our diet is lighter and is composed of much more processed food than at the turn of the century. The technological advances in the production and distribution of food made during the second half of the nineteenth century have been pursued to unbelievable lengths over the last seventy years. During that time food manufacturing has mushroomed into a huge, world-wide activity, and manufactured food, in one form or another, now forms a significant part of our diet. A vast number of products, unimagined at the turn of the century, today fill the shelves of huge self-service food stores. Each day brings some new kind of delicacy onto the market as manufacturers strive to satisfy the ever-increasing demands of the fickle consumer. Variety and individual preference have replaced simple necessity as the principal criteria upon which the selection of food is based today. Convenience and speed of preparation have become important determinants in the purchase of food in a society which now provides its members with a greater amount of leisure time than ever before. The practice of dining out, formerly reserved for the well-to-do, now pervades all classes alike. Indeed, it has been estimated recently that, on average, we now spend between 6 and 8 per cent of our income on meals outside the home. The emphasis today is on the exotic, although the fashion for French cuisine, current during the Edwardian era, has lost ground in the wake of the growing popularity of Chinese, Indian, Italian, Greek and other foods. At a slightly less formal level, the traditional fish and chip shop still remains with us, but nowadays it is facing increasing competition from new-style 'take-away food bars', which have sprung up in recent years in large numbers throughout the country, serving a wide variety of ready-to-eat foods from Chinese curries to American hamburgers to cater for all tastes.

A hundred and fifty years ago Brillat Savarin wrote: 'Tell me what you eat: I will tell you what you are.'[9] The applicability of this statement to Edwardian Britain is undeniable. The inequalities in income which characterised that period were shamefully reflected in the diet of the various classes in society. Today our food reflects the demands of the affluent pleasure-seeking society in which we live. Yet to attempt to apply Brillat Savarin's aphorism at a more specific level today would present insuperable difficulties. That this is the case suggests that the transformation which has taken place in the diet of the British people since the turn of the century has been of a fundamental nature. It implies that this transformation cannot be viewed in isolation, but rather as an integral part of the trends taking place at a more general level in the economy and society of Britain. For that reason it is important to bear in mind the unifying economic and social factors underlying the several parts of the story of the British diet described in the following pages.

Bread: A Staple Under Attack

THE SUBJECT of bread, in one form or another, has a habit of appearing in history books with almost predictable regularity. Down through the ages the price of bread has served as a sensor of public opinion and for that reason has been a matter of traditional concern to a succession of governments in Britain. The Luddite, Chartist and Anti-Corn Law movements of the nineteenth century, for example, all originated during times of rising bread prices, while in more recent times growing discontent over soaring food prices has prompted the introduction of government subsidies to peg the price of bread at artificially low levels. The quality of bread, as much as the price, has also for long occupied the attention of politicians in Britain, a fact to which a long list of enactments governing its nature and composition, as well as the conditions of its sale, readily testifies.

The significance of bread, of course, stems from the unique position it has held in the diet of the British people for many centuries. Right up until the twentieth century it was the single most important element—'the staff of life'— in the diet of the majority of the population of Britain, and this ubiquity through the ages has made it an important indicator of economic, social and political trends. Over the past hundred years or so, however, the role of bread has changed considerably. The major feature of this change has been a steady downward trend in consumption, interrupted only by the two world wars of the present century and directly related to the profound changes which have taken place in the economy and society of Britain since the latter decades of the nineteenth century.

Around the middle of the nineteenth century bread accounted for approximately one-third of the total expenditure on food in Britain. At that time, according to John Burnett, it was 'undoubtedly the staple of life for the 80 or 90 per cent of the population that made up the working classes. Often enough, it was practically the total diet, supplemented by tiny quantities of butter, cheese, bacon and tea.'[1] From the 1850s onwards the living standards of a large section of the population began to improve following the repeal of the Corn Laws in 1846. Average real wages began to rise as wheat prices declined, and during the next twenty years or so bread consumption, in fact, increased. However, although consumption was rising at this time, the share of bread in the diet of the working class was already beginning to decline, since a greater proportion of income was going towards the purchase of other products, which were becoming more readily available at prices which all but the poorest could afford. The so-called 'Great Depression' of the 1870s began a period of some twenty years during which the standard of living of the working class improved considerably. As massive quantities of cheap, imported foodstuffs came flooding onto the British market, the traditional dependence on bread was noticeably reduced. During this period the consumption of meat trebled, and that of a variety of other products including tea, cheese, fish, margarine and jam increased rapidly. By the turn of the century bread had already ceased to be the most important item of food expenditure for a great many families in Britain.

During the early years of the twentieth century, however, real wages began to decline once more in the wake of rising prices, and although the general trend of consumption continued to be downwards, for many working-class families bread once more assumed the premier position in their diet. For example, writing of his native Salford during this period, Robert Roberts recalled that in the poorest of households 'in bad times sauce on bread became the meal itself', while for the children of such families a 'sugar butty' or even a 'sweet tea leaf sandwich' would often represent a much-craved-for treat.[2] In the countryside too, if we recall for a moment the example of the agricultural labourer described in the previous chapter, who was devoting over half his family's food budget to the purchase of bread and flour, it is clear that at this time bread continued to occupy the prime position in the diet of a large section of the rural population of Britain.

The advent of the First World War in 1914 set the scene for a great increase in the consumption of bread. Throughout the four

B

years of fighting which followed, bread remained unrationed, and with other foods in short supply owing to the restrictions on imports, it once more established itself as the most important item in the diet of the majority of the British population. However, the ending of hostilities in 1918 signalled the opening of the flood-gates for a host of pent-up demands. The privations of war had created a thirst for variety, while at the same time the new-found affluence of a large section of the population, particularly women and teenagers, provided the means to satisfy these demands. The result was a spending spree which formed the basis of the im-mediate post-war boom in the economy of Britain. In such a climate, the consumption of bread was sure to suffer a setback, and although the boom soon gave way to a slump, the seeds of a mass-consumption society had been sown, in which variety rather than necessity was to become the major criterion in the choice of food.

Already by 1918, according to a report of the Working Classes' Cost of Living Committee of that year, when the general price of the four-pound loaf was 9d, the weekly expenditure on bread and flour by a standard family had fallen to 6s 9½d or 14·4 per cent of the total weekly expenditure on food excluding drink and tobacco. Throughout the inter-war years the consumption of bread barely kept pace with the increase in population, and although it must have continued to form the major part of the working-class diet in those areas where unemployment rates were highest when the Depression was at its worst, for that section of the population who were fortunate enough to remain in work, bread was taking increasingly less of the weekly food budget than before the war. Consumption per head of the population, which had stood at about 270 lb per year in the 1880s, had already fallen to approximately 197 lb per year by the mid-thirties and would have declined even further but for the outbreak of war in 1939. During the Second World War, as in the First, bread once more became the most freely available of all foods, and with con-sumption per head rising to over 230 lb per year, it once again became the most important item in the diet of the population. After the end of the war, however, the decline set in once more, and by 1960 the annual average consumption of bread had fallen to 170 lb. By 1973, with each person spending an average of just over 15½np on bread, and consuming an average of under 110 lb each year, it accounted for only about 6 per cent of total expenditure on food; a far cry from the 33 per cent of the mid-nineteenth century. So clearly the decline in both the absolute and the relative share of bread in the diet of the British population has been of considerable magnitude and calls for some explanation.

In the simplest of terms, the diminishing significance of bread reflects the steadily rising living standards of the majority of people in Britain since the end of the nineteenth century. The consumption of bread has traditionally been inversely related to the standards of living, for according to what economists describe as 'Engel's Law', the better off people are, the less they spend on basic foods, the most important of which is bread. This has undoubtedly been the case over the past hundred years. The steady rise in the purchasing power of a large section of the British population during the latter decades of the nineteenth century and later during the inter-war period meant that an increasing number of people could afford some choice of what they might eat, and, as a result, the demand for bread suffered. As living standards continued to improve rapidly after the Second World War, the demand for variety in diet intensified and the decline of bread became so pronounced that by the mid-sixties it had already come to occupy only a minor position in the diet of a large section of the population.

However, a number of other forces have been in operation which have also exercised a considerable influence on the pattern of bread consumption since the turn of the century. In fact, the changing role of bread over this period can be seen as a reflection of the dramatic changes which have taken place in the economic, social and occupational structure of Britain during the course of the twentieth century. The spread of mechanisation into every imaginable field of activity, by alleviating much of the former burden of manual labour associated with industry in the past, has reduced to a great extent the need for the high levels of consumption of such basic energy-giving foods as bread which character-ised the Victorian and Edwardian eras. The introduction of works canteens during the First World War and the rapid growth in their numbers thereafter was another important development affecting the consumption of bread, in so far as it discouraged the age-old practice among working men of taking a packed lunch to work. But perhaps the most important factor assisting the wane in the popularity of bread has been the steady growth in the ranks of the middle class over the last seventy years. Bread has, of course, always figured less prominently in the diet of the middle class than in that of the working class. However, during the twentieth century, as the proportion of the former in the total population has steadily increased, and as the tendency among this class to consume lighter and more frequent meals has become more pronounced, the overall consumption of bread has diminished at a faster rate than otherwise might have been expected.

A more specific explanation of the decline in the consumption of bread, which was advanced most strongly during the inter-war years in particular, associated the decline with the experience of the so-called 'war loaf'. During the First World War, owing to the disruption of normal trade, imports were seriously curtailed, and in view of the resulting food shortages the government ordered that the extraction rate of flour, that is, the proportion of the wheat which is actually converted into flour, should be raised from the normal pre-war level of approximately 70 per cent. The first of this war bread was of 76 per cent extraction, but economic stringency during the course of the war necessitated further increments in the extraction rate until, by the end of 1917, it stood at about 92 per cent. In addition, as the food situation deteriorated, the government ordered that soya, potato and other cereal flours should be added to the wheaten flour in order to make the most of available supplies of wheat. Although a perfectly valid economic measure, the raising of the extraction rate, however, had the unfortunate effect of providing flour which, when baked, produced a dark-coloured and foul-tasting loaf of bread which was detested by a population by now accustomed to light white bread. This war bread, so the argument goes, was directly responsible for the growing aversion of a large section of the British population, particularly children, towards bread during the inter-war period. In the words of one victim of war bread,

> Now of all the minor evils of the Great War, the loaf of this period may fairly claim front rank. It is more depressing than the plague of darkness and infinitely more dangerous than the air raids. One could hope to escape being hit by German bombs, but who could dodge the bullet-proof crust and sour soggy interior of a war loaf.[3]

The fact that this foul-tasting bread was unrationed throughout the four years of war and was therefore the most readily available of all foods, ensured that it became the major item in the diet of the majority of the British population. However, with the resumption of normal trade at the end of the war, it was inevitable that there would be a falling-off in the demand for bread as people began to satisfy pent-up demands for foods which had been scarce since the outbreak of hostilities. The growing popularity of sweets and chocolates probably had more to do with the decline in bread consumption among children than any-thing else during the inter-war years, and in general, the experi-ence of war bread had much less lasting effect on the long-term trend of bread consumption than has been suggested by its critics. The question, however, does raise another interesting subject, in so far as there existed a body of opinion in the country which actually favoured the retention of the higher extraction rate after the war on purely nutritional grounds. In fact, this divergence of opinion on the matter simply represented another instance in the age-old controversy associated with the colour of bread.

The colour of bread has been a contentious subject for many centuries. Indeed, two authors of a recent book on bread have gone so far as to suggest that 'If it is possible to condense 3,000 years of history into a few lines of print, the best way to do so is perhaps to consider the various groups who have pressed for bread to be brown or white.'[4] In the past the consumption of white bread was regarded as a mark of social superiority, for although it was universally desired, it was available only to those who could afford the expense involved in the long and tedious process of refining the flour. The majority of the population who made up the working class had to make do with dark, wholemeal bread, made from a variety of materials, including rye, oats and even beans, mixed with wheat. Although by the early nineteenth century bread made exclusively from wheat was being consumed by the majority of the population, the backwardness in milling methods meant that white bread was still only possible at great expense or, alternatively, by means of adulteration of the flour. Faced with the continuing demands for whiter bread, bakers were forced to resort to artificial means in order to improve the white-ness of their bread. The most commonly used additives were chemicals such as alum, chalk and ammonium carbonate, al-though bakers were frequently accused of employing other more dubious ingredients including ground stone, gypsum, pipe-clay and even powdered bones.

Around the middle of the nineteenth century, however, the introduction of silk gauze for the sifting of flour, in place of the woollen or linen fabrics previously used, enabled millers to produce a somewhat finer flour. But it was not until the 1870s that the real breakthrough came and a means was found of producing fine white flour cheaply and efficiently. The innovation which brought this about was the roller-mill. In this new type of mill, the first of which was established in Glasgow in 1872, the grain was passed through a series of rollers instead of being ground between flat stones as in the past. The new process meant that henceforth the bran and a large proportion of the greyish-yellow-coloured wheat germ could be sifted off, leaving a flour whiter than ever before possible by natural means. The introduction of roller-milling on a widespread scale also meant that, for the first time, bread made from fine white flour was cheaper to produce than that made from wholemeal. From this time on, white bread ceased to be a symbol of social superiority. Indeed, by the early years of the present century, white bread and tea, which had also formerly been a luxury enjoyed only by the rich, had already become associated more with those living below the poverty line than with the well-to-do. By the 1920s it was estimated that over 95 per cent of the total population were consuming white bread, and, in fact, by this time the consumption of brown wholemeal bread, now the more expensive of the two, had achieved a certain snob value among the better-off sections of society. The results of a dietary survey carried out during the thirties by Sir William Crawford and published under the title *The People's Food* (1938) revealed that a complete reversal had taken place in the pattern of bread consumption in Britain since the middle of the nineteenth century. According to this survey, consumption of wholemeal bread accounted for only 8·6 per cent of total bread consumption. A breakdown of consumption as between different classes in society showed that for the two upper classes (AA and A) the ratios of brown bread to white in the diet were 1 to 3·7 and 1 to 4·1 respectively; for the two lower classes (C and D) the ratios were 1 to 15·1 and 1 to 28·7 respectively. These findings provided a clear indication of the extent of the change which had taken place since the introduction of roller-milling.

Successful as it was in satisfying the age-old demand for white bread, the introduction of roller-milling, nevertheless, sparked off a controversy which has raged ever since and of which the 'war bread' argument is just one example. The controversy is centred around the relative merits of the traditional wholemeal bread and of the new bread made from roller-milled flour from which has been extracted, say the critics, many of the nutritional qualities of the wheat in order to satisfy the demand for white bread. To press the claims of the former, the Bread and Food Reform League was established by May Yates in 1880, while a number of other apostles of wholemeal bread, the most notable of whom were Sylvester Graham and Dr T. R. Allinson, drew attention to the dangers of bread made from roller-milled flour. The arguments, however, often tended to be rather unscientific, and as a result the brown bread campaigners came to be regarded as cranks by many people. Allinson, for example, claimed that brown bread was 'the true staff of life—one which would not break under people' and which would equip children with the necessary strength to fight their way through the world. White bread, on the other hand, often led people to suffer from 'an inward craving or sinking' to satisfy which they were likely to resort to drink. Consequently, 'if they ate brown bread they would not suffer from this and we should be a soberer nation'.[5]

Despite these claims, and despite the fact that the baking trade responded to them by producing a number of tasty wholemeal breads, the most famous of which was Hovis,* white bread continued to gain in popularity. Most people preferred it, and it was cheaper and easier to obtain. Apart from this, however, the fact remained that no sound medical evidence existed which could prove that white bread was injurious to health. In fact, the results of a number of scientific investigations showed complete unanimity in agreeing that white bread contained more protein and more calories than did brown. However, the discovery of vitamins in 1912 provided the proponents of brown bread with new scientific evidence to support their claims, since it was proven that bread made from wholemeal flour contained greater amounts of vitamins B_1 and B_2 (thiamine and riboflavin respectively) than that

* These were, however, not like old wholemeal bread baked from coarse wholemeal flours, but simply bread baked from roller-milled white flour mixed with various proportions of bran.

made from flour of low extraction rate produced by the roller-milling process.

During the First World War the debate was pushed into the background as the exigencies of war called for the production of the wholemeal 'war loaf' which everyone was required to suffer alike. With the cessation of hostilities and the end of food control, the debate was renewed once more with even greater vigour on the part of the proponents of the brown loaf. National and local newspapers throughout the inter-war years regularly carried headlines either in support of or opposed to wholemeal bread. One such headline in the *Daily Mail* read:

'THE WHITER YOUR BREAD THE SOONER YOU'RE DEAD',

while on the other side of the fence a Hull journal assured its readers that

'WHITE BREAD'S BEST, BROWN WON'T DIGEST'.

During the twenties, campaigns by various groups of food faddists became commonplace, in the course of which the consumption of white bread was associated with all kinds of ailments including cancer, tuberculosis, appendicitis and even mental disorder.

The controversy reached boiling-point when it was discovered that millers were treating their flour with 'improvers' to increase its keeping qualities, and with bleaching agents to make it even whiter. It seemed that the demand for pure white bread was not being satisfied by simple roller-milling, since the flour produced by this process was still a very pale cream colour. Incensed by this discovery, the Bread and Food Reform League immediately demanded that the government should 'take measures to prevent the abstraction without notification to the public from wholemeal, wheatmeal and household flour, of the germ of wheat and gluten in flours commercially designated patents and also to prevent the sale without notification to the public of flour which has been bleached, improved or otherwise adulterated';[6] while another leading body in the anti-white movement, the New Health Society, called for a national consumers' bread strike. In 1926 the president of this organisation, Sir William Arbuthnot Lane, referred in a speech to white bread as 'the curse of the age'. He claimed that 'The milling process to which our foods are subjected is one of the worst things civilised man has devised for his own undoing. Deliberately to remove certain parts of the wheat grain so as to please the eye and the palate, while we rob the body of the invaluable material for its well-being is surely the height of folly.'[7]

The Millers' Association, confronted with this flood of criticism, replied with facts and figures. They produced the results of a survey which they had carried out in 1926 among a thousand doctors throughout the country, concerning the relative merits of white and brown bread. These results revealed that 89 per cent of the doctors in the sample actually ate white bread themselves, 76·6 per cent repudiated Sir William Arbuthnot Lane's statement that white bread was the curse of the age, and 80·1 per cent regarded white bread as good nutritious food in a mixed diet. In reply to the critics of the artificial treatment of flour, Sir William Jago, one of the foremost authorities on bread and flour at the time, stated categorically that the treatment of flour with persulphates did not result in any detriment to the public and that, in fact, as a consequence of it, people were supplied with a pure loaf of better flavour and great digestibility and consequently higher nutritive value. His claim was given official backing by the publication of the report of a departmental committee of the Ministry of Health which had investigated the whole question of the treatment of flour with chemical substances. Perhaps the most significant conclusion reached in this report was that 'So long as a great demand exists in this country for very white bread, some form of bleaching process must be permitted.'[8] However, on purely economic grounds the committee also pointed out that improvers in flour had been of great assistance to British millers in competition with those from overseas and that prohibition of their use might be prejudicial to home producers.

Despite all this evidence in support of white bread, and despite the fact that it was almost universally consumed and liked, the controversy continued unabated until the outbreak of war in 1939, when once again the British population were required to endure a 'war loaf', or, as it was called on this occasion, a 'national loaf' made from flour of 85 per cent extraction. The ending of hostilities in 1945 did not signal the end of the 'national loaf' which in fact remained on the market until 1953. The reason for the delay in the return to normality was partly due to economic stringency, but it was also due in part to the desire of the government to devise a sound nutritional policy centred around a loaf of the highest nutritional value. However, in the meantime new evidence was brought to light which re-kindled the white *versus* brown debate. The first of this new evidence was produced by Sir Edward Mellanby, a well-known and respected research physician, who drew attention in the early forties to the practice of bleaching flour with the substance nitrogen trichloride, more commonly known as agene, which had been in use in most British flourmills since the twenties. Mellanby revealed that some test dogs fed on a diet composed of bread made from agenised flour developed running fits. Although no evidence was produced to suggest that agene could have the same effect on humans, Mellanby's revelations caused enough stir in government circles to result in the banning of this substance in 1955.

But perhaps the most important advance in the debate came with the publication in 1954 of a report on a series of feeding experiments carried out shortly after the war on a group of children living in two orphanages, one in Duisburg and one in Wuppertal, two neighbouring towns in Germany. The general objective of these experiments was 'to find out everything possible about the nutritional value of bread, variously milled or enriched, as a food for man'. In the course of the experiments, the children, some 250 in all, were divided into groups and each group was allowed a diet which contained unlimited supplies of a specific type of bread from a selection which included 100 per cent wholemeal, bread of 80 per cent extraction, of 70 per cent extraction and of 70 per cent extraction enriched with various nutrients. The results of the experiments showed clearly that the children in the different groups, consuming different types of bread, all developed at the same rate from an initially equal state of undernourishment. This seemed to prove conclusively that bread made from white unenriched flour was just as valuable a constituent of diet as bread made from wholemeal flour.

Despite this strong evidence in support of white bread, the government was not convinced. When the milling industry was eventually freed from wartime control in 1953, it was under the condition that where flour of less than 80 per cent extraction was produced, synthetic nutrients should be added so as to make the flour as if milled of 80 per cent extraction. Three years later, in 1956, the Panel on the Composition and Nutritive Value of Flour which had been set up by the government under the chairmanship of Professor Henry Cohen, produced its report. In this document it was suggested that flour of 70 per cent extraction which had been enriched with synthetic nutrients was as nutritious a food as flour of 80 per cent extraction. And acting on the recommendations of this report, the government made it its official policy that flour of less than 80 per cent extraction should be enriched or 'fortified' by the addition of iron, chalk and vitamins B_1 and B_2 in order to compensate for the loss of these nutrients in the milling process.

The fortification of flour, of course, provided the anti-white campaigners with further ammunition with which to keep the debate a live issue. Indeed, in recent years, no less than in the past, complaints about the quality of bread in Britain have been numerous, and they have not diminished with the decline in the overall consumption of bread. Nevertheless, as in the past, the calls for a return to wholemeal bread, free from any form of chemical treatment, have fallen on deaf ears, for the fact remains that the overwhelming majority of the population, whatever their thoughts on the chemical treatment of bread, prefer it to be as white as possible and to have a palatable taste. Whether in fact there is a case for a return to wholemeal bread on purely nutritional grounds is also doubtful, despite the arguments in favour of such a move. The fact is that in today's affluent society, bread has long since ceased to be the primary source of nutriment for the majority of the population; as one writer has said recently, 'It is unlikely that differences in the bread we eat are at all relevant in the content of our diet as a whole. Unless new evidence is found, it seems that the colour problem for bread is a myth, not of course that this means that there are no differences between different types of bread, only that the differences are not significant.'[9] Whether we like it or not, white bread is here to stay.

Although the consumption of bread has been declining since the latter decades of the nineteenth century, that of several other grain-based products, including breakfast cereals, biscuits and cakes, has grown steadily since that time. Indeed, the growing popularity of these products has had more than a little to do with the reduced consumption of bread in many households in Britain.

Breakfast cereals, which originated in the United States during the second half of the nineteenth century, had already found their way onto the shelves of grocery stores in Britain by the outbreak of war in 1914. Force, Grape Nuts and Malta Vita, all imported from America, were among the first to appear on the British market. However, before the war the consumption of these products was negligible, and it was not until the inter-war years that breakfast cereals began to make a serious impact on the British consumer. During the twenties products such as Corn Flakes, Shredded Wheat, Puffed Wheat and Rice Krispies quickly rose to prominence as the big American cereal manufacturers Kelloggs, Nabisco and Quaker established factories for their production in Britain. The only major British firm to emerge during the inter-war period was Weetabix, which began operations, under the name of the African Cereal Company, in 1932. Backed by dynamic advertising campaigns, breakfast cereals soon found widespread popularity among the middle class. However, by 1938, with the consumption per head at under $1\frac{1}{2}$ oz per week, they were still in their infancy, and it was only after 1945, with rising living standards among the working class, that they began to gain universal popularity. By 1960 each household in Britain was already spending an estimated 1s $4\frac{1}{2}$d (7np) on cereals each week. During the sixties consumption expanded rapidly, and by 1973, with each person consuming an average weekly amount of 2·95 oz, expenditure had risen to 14np.

With the increasing emphasis on tasty and convenient foods since the end of the First World War, the demand for bread has been even more seriously affected by the growing consumption of biscuits and cakes. Consumption of these products has increased so much over the last fifty years that today they account for as great a share of total food expenditure in Britain as does bread itself. Neither, however, are twentieth-century discoveries. The biscuit, for example, is said to have a long and distinguished history, which one writer was moved to expound during the twenties in the following words:

There is an epic in the march of a biscuit, side by side with man. No ship dare sail, says our legislative assembly, without a goodly store of biscuits; no army dare fight without them. The Arctic explorer desperately cheers the dogs through the eternal snow as they drag the precious sledge laden with the biscuit boxes. In the heart of the jungle, where brooding silence is broken by the fierce cry of the ravenous beast, the explorer kneels close to the fire to open his airtight biscuit tin. The scarlet clad huntsman munches biscuits as his blown steed rests beneath the oak tree in the lane. The crag climber, with fingers numbed by fingerholds in the sensational traverse, leans back for a moment with his biscuit. The rambler, joyous on the foot-path way, finds them the food of the gods. Restless, adventur-ous man, pioneer and explorer, mastering reluctant earth, wresting its secrets from its heart; and the biscuit has been in at every victory. It has been with the submarine, in the airship and it will climb Everest yet. The epic of the biscuit has yet to be written. The adventures of virile men, the loving care of homely women, the innocent mischief of the child, biscuits are at home with them all.[10]

However, the biscuit as we know it today only really came into existence during the second half of the nineteenth century. This followed the introduction of machinery which enabled the production of 'fancy' biscuits in large quantities and of standard quality. Before that time the most commonly known form of biscuit was the ship's biscuit which was carried on board most ocean-going vessels as a convenient substitute for bread. In fact, an early definition of the biscuit specifically described it as 'a kind of hard dry bread made to be carried at sea'.[11] The production of biscuits for domestic use before the middle of the nineteenth century was carried out on a very small scale and under the most primitive of conditions. Many bakers at the time simply regarded it as a profitable sideline to their main business of baking bread. During the second half of the nineteenth century, however, large-scale mechanisation brought about a dramatic change in the traditional image of the biscuit.

The evolution of the biscuit industry into its modern form owed much to the enterprise of Jonathan Dodgson Carr, who during the 1830s adopted mechanical means to speed up the processes of preparation and baking in his biscuit factory at Carlisle. For this purpose he designed a machine on the principle of the old printing-press, which would cut out the biscuit paste more readily than by hand, and it is on the basis of this invention that Carlisle has ever since strongly upheld its claim to being 'the birthplace of the biscuit industry'. Huntley & Palmers of Reading, however, refute this claim, pointing out that they were the first to introduce the travelling oven into their factory and so were the pioneers of modern biscuit manufacture, while yet another firm, William Crawfords, founded in 1813, lay claim to being 'the oldest of biscuit manufacturers'. Whichever of these firms was first into the field of mechanised biscuit production (the evidence would seem to support the claim of Carrs of Carlisle), they were soon followed by a number of rivals including McVitie & Price, Peek Frean, MacFarlane Lang and Jacobs, all household names today.

By the outbreak of the First World War the biscuit had already become an important item in the diet of the middle class. During the inter-war years it began to make an impact on the diet of the working class as competition between biscuit manufacturers resulted in a steady reduction in prices while increased mechanisation led to improvement in quality and to a rapid increase in the variety of biscuits available. Consumption more than trebled as prices fell from an average of over 2s to 10d per pound between 1920 and 1938. There also grew up during this period a group of cut-price biscuit manufacturers which included the Co-operative Wholesale Society and Kemps International, who began to sell biscuits for as little as 6d per pound. By 1935, with over 240,000 tons of biscuits being produced each year in Britain, the industry was split into two factions. On the one hand were the old-established firms who continued to produce biscuits for the 'quality' end of the market; on the other were the low-cost, low-price producers who were turning out a large variety of cheap biscuits which were gaining widespread popularity among the lower income groups. After the wartime interruption to trade, the demand for biscuits re-established a steadily rising trend. By 1956 the output of biscuits in Britain had increased to over 500,000 tons, and this upward trend has continued ever since.

The great rise in living standards since 1945 has so radically altered the dietary pattern of the majority of the British population that the biscuit has come to assume a much greater importance in the diet of a great many people. The growing habit of consuming fewer and lighter meals has led to the development of the 'snack' industry to meet the demand for tasty and convenient 'fillers', of which the biscuit is a prime example. By 1973 it was estimated that each person in Britain was consuming an average of about $5\frac{1}{2}$ oz of biscuits every week; chocolate biscuits accounted for over a quarter of this amount. The success of this latter branch of the biscuit industry since 1945 has been remarkable, and it owes much to the enterprise of one company, Macdonalds.

Although a number of firms were producing a range of chocolate-coated biscuits before 1939, it was not until after the war that this activity was turned into a lucrative business in its own right. The initiative in this direction came from William and Frank Macdonald, who operated a small biscuit-making concern in Glasgow. They decided that rather than try to compete with the big companies on their own terms, they would instead specialise their production on a small range of high-quality, chocolate-coated products. They also decided to break with tradition by advertising the individual product on its own merit instead of using the name of the company as in the past. The first, and still the most famous, product to be launched in this fashion was the 'Penguin'. Its success was immediate, and so too was the success of Macdonalds, who followed up the Penguin with a number of other equally well-known biscuits, such as 'Yo-yo', 'Munch-mallow', 'Bandit' and 'Taxi', all of which gained widespread popularity as tea-time snacks. By 1956, with an output of over 18,000 tons in that year, it was estimated that Macdonalds were producing almost a quarter of all fully-coated chocolate biscuits in Britain. And during the sixties they led the way as the popularity of this type of product continued to increase steadily. The removal of purchase tax from chocolate biscuits in March 1973 gave an important boost to consumption, and by the end of that year the average weekly expenditure on chocolate biscuits was nearly $2\frac{1}{2}$np per person.

Increasing affluence during the course of the twentieth century has also stimulated the demand for a wide range of flour confectionery including cakes, pastries, buns, scones and teacakes, and over the past half century production of these delicacies has developed into a large-scale business operated both by specialised firms and by a number of biscuit manufacturers as a profitable sideline. During the inter-war period, with prices declining rapidly as a result of the introduction of mechanised production methods, consumption of these products almost doubled, and after 1945 the upward trend continued, with the traditional bread and flour confectioners coming under increasing pressure from the specialist cake producers, who were now beginning to turn out standardised and pre-packaged products on a large scale. By 1965 the average weekly consumption per person of flour confectionery in Britain had reached 6·7 oz. However, the demand for this type of product then began to taper off as the range of cheap and tasty convenience foods steadily expanded. By 1973 the average weekly consumption had fallen to less than 5 oz per person, and hand in hand with this decline in the popularity of flour confectionery, the consumption of self-raising and patent flours also began to exhibit a noticeable downward trend, falling from an average of 6·5 oz per person per week in 1963 to 5·25 oz ten years later in 1973. This clearly reflected the fact that although the practice of baking flour confectionery at home was still common, it was, by the sixties, definitely on the decline.

The home baking of bread had by this time, of course, virtually disappeared, except in some isolated areas of the country. However, the decline in this practice did not follow a universal pattern. Certainly in most areas of the country the change to commercially baked bread had taken place long before the end of the nineteenth century, as the introduction of machinery such as flour sifters, dough kneaders and dividers, and finally the travelling oven, made possible, for the first time, the large-scale factory production of bread. During the inter-war period further refinements in the process of mechanical baking, culminating in the introduction of wrapping during the twenties and slicing during the thirties, virtually completed the shift to commercially baked bread throughout the country. In a few areas, however, the age-old custom of baking one's own bread remained in vogue until well into the twentieth century. The north-east of England was the bastion of the practice. It was estimated, for example, in 1919 that some 69 per cent of all bread consumed in Newcastle and 67 per cent of that consumed in Leeds at the time was home-baked, while only 8 per cent and 7 per cent was baked at home in London and Glasgow respectively. During the Depression, with unemployment in the North-East among the highest in the country, the practice remained firmly entrenched, and it was only after the Second World War, with the retail price of flour steadily rising and with the growth of bakery firms with national distribution networks (such as Allied Bakeries), that the home-baked loaf began to lose ground rapidly.

Increasing mechanisation in the baking trade ultimately led to a growth in the importance of large-scale plants in the production of bread and, consequently, to a growth in the size of firms in the trade. Between 1935 and 1955 the proportion of bread produced in plants in Britain rose from 5 per cent to 37 per cent, and hand in hand with this trend several huge bakery firms emerged, producing bread for the national market. The first nationally branded loaf was 'Wonderloaf', introduced in 1953 by Spillers. This was soon followed by 'Sunblest' (Allied Bakeries), 'Wheatsheaf' (Co-operative Wholesale Society and retail societies) and later, by 'Mothers Pride' (Rank Hovis McDougall). By 1965 these four brands between them accounted for over 40 per cent of the total market for wrapped and sliced bread. And through a series of amalgamations and takeovers during the fifties and sixties, the four companies producing them came to dominate the market for bread in Britain : by 1969 they were responsible for some 70 per cent of the total sales of bread.

While these large firms were growing to pre-eminence, the small master baker steadily declined in importance. As consumer preference swung strongly towards the convenience of wrapped and sliced bread, the craftsman baker, producing a range of traditional products, found himself increasingly at a serious competitive disadvantage to the larger plant operators. As a result, many were forced out of business, and during the twenty-five years after the Second World War membership of the National Association of Master Bakers fell by some 5,000. However, in recent years there has been a revival in the demand for hot crusty bread, to the production of which the small bakery is better suited than the large plants of the major firms. This has enabled the small master baker to hold his own against the competition of the national brands; and indeed, recognising this trend, one of the big four, Allied Bakeries, has already spent a considerable amount of money in equipping its retail outlets with the machinery to produce crusty bread for sale hot from the oven.[12]

Despite these developments, the overall decline in the consumption of bread continues. Through further concentration and increasing sophistication in production and marketing techniques, bakers can only hope to consolidate existing shares of the dwindling market. Most have already diversified extensively into the production of biscuits, cakes and other types of convenience snacks, and only the most optimistic could fail to recognise that bread has abdicated its premier position in the British diet for ever.

From Farm to Factory: The Development of Food Manufacturing in Britain

DURING the course of the nineteenth century there was a continuous drift of people from the countryside into the towns to supply labour for the rapidly expanding industrial sector. This movement, together with the high natural rate of growth of the population as a whole, produced a continuous increase in the size of the urban population of Britain. The number of people living in the Greater London area, for example, which stood at just over one million in 1801, trebled over the course of the next sixty years, and doubled again during the last forty years of the nineteenth century. Manchester, with a population of only 75,000 in 1801, was already by 1861 a city of over half a million inhabitants, while other towns such as Birmingham, Liverpool and Glasgow experienced similar growth in numbers. In all, by the turn of the century over three-quarters of the population of Britain were town-dwellers.

This dramatic upsurge in the urban population presented a number of serious problems, for by the middle of the nineteenth century large numbers of these urban labourers and their families were living in appallingly overcrowded and insanitary conditions. One of the greatest problems which the spread of urbanisation threw up in its wake was that of feeding the vastly increased numbers. Before the arrival of the railways, the fact that such a large proportion of the population lived so far from the sources of food production meant that food in towns was expensive and was, more often than not, already in a state of decay by the time it had travelled from farm to town. Under such conditions, for the majority of the urban working class at this time a diet of bread, potatoes and tea, supplemented occasionally by small quantities of bacon, had to suffice.

During the second half of the nineteenth century, however,

the standard of living of the working class in Britain improved considerably. The removal of the Corn Laws in 1846 signalled the advent of Free Trade and heralded an era of industrial and commercial expansion. Between 1850 and 1870 the demand for labour was brisk, and although food prices were rising, money wages more than kept pace, allowing, for the first time, a large section of the working class some margin above subsistence. In addition, the development of the railway network from the late 1840s onwards alleviated the problem of food transportation, and helped bring a greater variety of foodstuffs within reach of the urban working class. The most important breakthrough, however, came after 1870. During and after the so-called 'Great Depression' of the latter decades of the century imports of cheap meat, wheat, fruit, sugar, etc. in large quantities led to considerable reductions in the prices of these commodities. As a result, the real purchasing power of a large section of the British population increased noticeably. For the first time many working-class families could afford to have a choice of what they might eat, a fact which stimulated into action those engaged in the production and distribution of food. In this climate the application of science and technology to the business of food production began to proceed at a rapid rate; and before the end of the century an industry of considerable magnitude had grown up to cope with the problem of manufacturing, preserving, transporting and selling an increasing variety of foods to a rapidly expanding market.

Before the First World War, however, only the tip of the iceberg had been revealed and the enormous potential of the factory production of foods was only just becoming apparent. Since then, of course, the business of food manufacture has mushroomed dramatically, both in size and sophistication. Today almost every food imaginable is produced in a manufactured form, and in fact processed food in one form or another accounts for the major part of the modern British diet. The First World War was an important catalyst in this direction. It gave a great stimulus to the large-scale factory production of a number of food products. Import restrictions during the four years of war led to intensive technical investigation into numerous methods of preparation, preservation and storage of foods, while the need for co-ordination and co-operation led to a greater degree of concentration in the organisation of the food manufacturing industry.

The developments in the production and distribution of manu-factured foods which occurred during and before the war pro-vided the foundation upon which the manufacturers of food successfully built during the inter-war years. A steadily expanding market, composed of consumers already becoming more discern-ing in their choice of foods, provided the stimulus towards growth and change within the food manufacturing industry. The trend towards mechanisation and rationalisation in production methods resulted in a greater emphasis on the standardisation of products, which in turn led to the transference of many of the food retailer's traditional functions to the manufacturer, while, at the same time, much greater attention was being paid to the business of market-ing and distribution. Practices such as the branding of goods and resale price maintenance came into vogue and led to an un-precedented emphasis on packaging and advertising. In fact, by 1939 the food manufacturing industry was rapidly developing into the form we know today. The Second World War stimulated further investigation into problems associated with the factory production of a number of foods, and the growth and diversifica-tion of the food manufacturing industry since 1945 owes much to the discoveries of food scientists involved in wartime research.

The post-war era has seen the consumption of manufactured foods increase at an astonishing rate. Rising living standards have led to increased demands for variety in diet, while the pursuit of pleasure has led to a greater emphasis being placed on the idea of labour-saving in the preparation of food. This is reflected in the growing importance of the 'convenience' element in the business of food production. 'Quick-frozen', 'freeze-dried', 'ready-made' and 'instant' are all terms which were unknown seventy years ago, for they are products of the fast-moving world in which we live today. They reflect not only our changing attitudes to food but also the great changes which have taken place in the British way of life during the course of the twentieth century.

The growth in the manufacture of convenience foods has in fact been one of the most striking features of the last fifteen years. Between 1963 and 1968, for example, expenditure on conveni-ence foods rose by an estimated 30 per cent, nearly twice as much as expenditure on food as a whole over the same period. And the trend has continued ever since, so that today they already account for a quarter of all expenditure on food in Britain. From the simple tin of pre-cooked vegetables to the complete ready-made meal, convenience foods pervade the diet of all classes alike. By effectively shifting the locus of much of the cooking and preparation of food from home to factory, they have removed much of the drudgery from housework. In so doing, both as a response to the growing desire of women to work outside the home, and as part and parcel of the more general trend towards labour-saving in the home, they have played no small part in the liberation of women over the past few decades. And for those thousands of inhabitants of the 'bedsitter lands' of our big cities, they have become an indispensable part of daily living, satisfying the dual needs for economy and hygiene. In the field of mass catering also, the remarkable trend towards the greater use of manufactured convenience foods in recent years has injected new life into an industry renowned in the past for its poor standards and lack of imagination in menus. In a total of over 40,000 restaurants, cafés, snack bars, etc. throughout the country today, a greater selection of food than ever before, much of it pre-cooked, pre-packaged and ready to serve, has done much to create a new image for the catering industry.

The development of the food manufacturing industry has undoubtedly been one of the most outstanding features of the twentieth century; its effect on the diet and, indeed, the lives of the British people has been overwhelming. The history of this development is one of many parts, each of which requires some consideration. In its earliest and simplest form the business of food manufacture involved the introduction of machinery and the application of new techniques of mass-production to existing processes. The result of this was normally a reduction in the price of the article and the loss of its 'luxury' tag. The introduction of roller-milling, discussed earlier, was a classic example of this; it led to a fall in the price of white bread which, formerly reserved for the better-off sections of the community, became available to the working class for the first time. The introduction of machinery into the process of biscuit manufacture had the same effect of reducing the price of biscuits and widening the circle of consumers, and the same was particularly true of the chocolate industry.

Until the late nineteenth century chocolate was consumed in Britain exclusively by the aristocracy. In fact its introduction to

England during the seventeenth century marked the very peak in snobbishness, for within a short time of its arrival the habit of using chocolate was deemed a token of elegant and fashionable taste. An entry in the renowned diary of Samuel Pepys in November 1664 reads: 'To a coffee house to drink jocolatte—very good,' and indeed, chocolate-houses, the first of which was opened in 1657 by a Frenchman in Queen's Head Alley in Bishopsgate, quickly replaced coffee-houses, opened only a few years earlier, as the rendezvous of the elite. During the seventeenth and eighteenth centuries, however, although chocolate had captured the imagination of society, it was still a subject of some controversy. To its admirers, it was a nectar, imbued with countless virtues; to its opponents, it was a curse, said to inflame the passion and overheat the body. In a verse written in 1667 Andrew Marvell bemoaned the poisoning of Lady Denham with a cup of chocolate, while 150 years later the eminent surgeon Lister was claiming that over-indulgence in chocolate caused apoplexy! Notwithstanding these objections, which probably did more than anything else to enhance the glamorous and mysterious aura which surrounded it, the consumption of chocolate increased steadily.

During this period all chocolate produced was for drinking purposes. It was not until after the first quarter of the nineteenth century that methods were introduced for moulding chocolate into a solid cake for eating. The exact date of the introduction of chocolate in this solid form is not known. The first reference to it was on a price-list issued by Cadbury Brothers in 1842. Significantly, the chocolate mentioned on this list was described as 'French'—evidence of the still luxurious associations. Frys, the oldest English firm of chocolate-makers, were certainly manufacturing eating chocolate in 1847 and may possibly have made it earlier. At any rate, methods of manufacture at this time were primitive by modern standards, and the duty on chocolate was so high that it remained within reach of only a small section of the population. Nevertheless, consumption was increasing, and by the time Gladstone fixed the duty on imported cacao beans at 1d in 1853 Britain was already importing over 1,400 tons of cacao beans each year, compared with less than 500 twenty years earlier. The reduction of the duty on cacao marks the turning-point in the history of the chocolate industry. Although it continued to be regarded as a rare and expensive luxury during the latter decades of the nineteenth century, imports of cheap cacao, sugar and fats all helped to bring the price of chocolate within range of a widening circle of consumers. This trend was clearly reflected in the growing imports of raw cacao, which rose to nearly 17,000 tons in 1900. It was also accelerated between 1870 and 1914 by the application of scientific and technological knowledge to the process of chocolate manufacture. During this period increasing demand for chocolate led to a flood of new techniques and machinery, which not only produced an improvement in the quality and a reduction in the price of traditional products, but also enabled the mass-production of a new range of products based on the use of milk chocolate.

Milk chocolate for eating was first produced in quantity by the firm of Peters of Vevey, in Switzerland, around the year 1876, and before the end of the century the Swiss, with such firms as Cailler and Nestlé, had a virtual monopoly of the market for milk chocolate in Britain. It was 1897 before a British firm, Cadbury Brothers, marketed a milk chocolate. However, it was a further eight years before a successful competitor against the popular Swiss brands was finally introduced in the shape of 'Cadbury's Dairy Milk'. Made with fresh, full-cream milk, this chocolate was much smoother-tasting than the darker Swiss varieties, and it gained an immediate foothold in the market. By the outbreak of war in 1914 the Swiss had lost their hold on the British chocolate market, which was now dominated by a trio of British firms. By this time, despite significant technological progress in its manufacture, chocolate was still relatively expensive and its consumption was by no means universal. However, during the First World War chocolate gained a great deal in popularity as a direct result of circumstances created by the war. Many thousands of men fighting abroad who had previously taken little interest in sweets now learnt from the use of their emergency rations that chocolate was a convenient and pleasant-tasting foodstuff. And at home, children, with other foods in short supply, soon developed a taste for it.

During the inter-war years this popularity quickly increased. The rapid spread of mechanisation in the chocolate industry and the steady decline in the prices of sugar and cacao resulted in a considerable fall in the cost of manufacturing chocolate. Simultaneously, increasing concentration within the industry wrought considerable economies of scale. The industry came to be dominated by a handful of firms, of which the largest were Cadburys of Bournville, Rowntrees of York and Frys of Bristol; and it was estimated that by 1938 six companies between them accounted for some 60 per cent of the total production of chocolate confectionery in Britain. The outcome of all these developments was that the price of a one-pound block of chocolate fell from nearly 4s in 1920 to 1s 4d in 1938; as a result, consumption increased steadily, with imports of raw cacao soaring to nearly 90,000 tons in 1938. By this time, with over 250,000 shops throughout the country selling sweets and chocolates, expenditure on these products stood at over £55 million, nearly two-thirds of which went on chocolate and chocolate confectionery.

This in fact represented not only a change in public taste but also a reversal in the traditional relationship between chocolate and sugar confectionery. Up until the last quarter of the nineteenth century sugar confectionery, i.e. toffee, boiled sweets, candied nuts, flavoured drops, etc., had been the big selling branch of the confectionery industry; chocolate accounted for only one-third of the total production of confectionery as late as 1900. Since that time, however, chocolate and chocolate confectionery have made continuous ground, much to the detriment of the sugar confectionery industry. However, most of the worst effects of the competition from chocolate products have been felt in the traditional branches of the sugar confectionery industry; several newer branches have been less affected and have fared considerably better than the industry as a whole. One such branch is that which produces chewing-gum.

Chewing-gum was an American invention. It was in 1871 that the first patent was taken out for a gum-making machine. This followed the discovery by an American called Adams of some chicle—a coagulated latex which forms the base of chewing-gum —which a Mexican friend had left behind after a visit to New York. Having tasted it and found it pleasant to chew, Adams decided to roll some of this chicle into strips and sell it to a sweet store in Jersey City. It was an immediate success, and Adams then set up a factory to manufacture chewing-gum on a commercial basis. After several refinements, including the addition of sugar and flavouring, chewing-gum became an important newcomer to the range of sweets then available in the United States. By the end of the century several large firms, including Wrigleys, who pioneered spearmint gum, and Beech Nut, were producing chewing-gum on a mass-production basis. It eventually came to Britain with soldiers returning from the First World War, who had had contact with American soldiers among whom the habit of chewing gum was already well entrenched. During the twenties the habit spread very quickly to other sections of the population; it was encouraged by extensive advertising on the part of Wrigleys and Beech Nut, who quickly came to dominate the British market; and by the outbreak of war in 1939 sales of chewing-gum in Britain were already in the region of about £1 million each year.

Other products, particularly fruit gums and pastilles, have also gained widespread popularity during the course of the twentieth century, once again owing mainly to extensive and dynamic advertising. Rowntrees of York were the pioneers in this field. It was in 1879 that this company decided to manufacture pastilles and gums, then a French monopoly. For this purpose they employed a Frenchman, Claude Gaget, and with two men, a boy and a boiling-pan he laid the foundations of a trade in which Rowntrees today stand predominant. Fruit pastilles were first introduced in 1883, but it was 1928 before they were first marketed as 'the sweets that men like (girls like them too)' in the now familiar tubes and cartons.

Since 1945 the chocolate and confectionery industry as a whole has not maintained the momentum it gained during the first half of the century. For most of the post-war period the average consumption of chocolate has tended to stagnate, while that of sugar confectionery has tapered off dramatically. This is in part due to the growth of the snack industry, which nowadays provides a wide variety of tasty and convenient sweet and savoury snacks which compete directly with the products of the confectionery industry; as such, it is a reflection of the increasing affluence of the majority of the population. Nevertheless, in absolute terms, consumption of confectionery has continued to rise since the end of the Second World War, and the fact remains that the consumption per head of sweets and chocolates in Britain today is still the highest in the world.

Apart from the modernisation of the methods of production

and the consequent reduction in the prices of a number of former luxury foods during the latter decades of the nineteenth century, the development of the food manufacturing industry also involved the introduction of several new products. Initially intended as cheap substitutes for fresh varieties, a number of these new products were to play an important role in the diet of the British population during the course of the twentieth century. One of them was margarine.

It was invented in France in 1869, following the promotion in that year of a competition between French chemists by Napoleon III, the purpose of which was to find a cheap substitute for butter. The inventor and winner of the award was a food technologist, Hippolyte Mège-Mouries. He produced an edible substitute for butter using a process by which it was possible to separate the oily from the solid part of the fat of a cow by pressing it between hot plates. The oily part, which melted at about the same temperature as butter, was called 'oleo' and formed the base of the new butter substitute. The finished product was made by churning the oleo with milk and cows' udders. Mège-Mouries' process was not, however, developed on a commercial basis in France. His patent was bought from him by a Dutch firm of butter merchants and was developed in the Netherlands. Before 1880 the Dutch were already exporting large quantities of this butter substitute, which was known at the time as 'butterine', to Britain. At the same time some American meat-packing concerns began producing their own brand of butterine and were soon exporting large quantities to Britain, as well as supplying the Dutch industry with huge quantities of the basic raw material, cow fat. The use of the name 'butterine', however, aroused violent opposition from the producers of butter in Britain and eventually its use was banned in 1887.

Once clearly distinguished from butter, margarine, contrary to the expectations of its critics, increased in popularity as a growing number of working-class housewives came to recognise its value as a cheap substitute for butter. Production did not commence in Britain until 1889, when the firm of Otto Monsted built a factory at Godley in Cheshire. However, by the outbreak of war in 1914, although the Dutch were still supplying almost half of Britain's requirements of margarine, an industry of considerable size had grown up in Britain, dominated by one large firm, the Maypole

Dairy Company (in conjunction with Monsteds), which was responsible for one-third of the total market for margarine in the United Kingdom. By this time margarine had become an integral part of the diet of the British working class. Indeed, as early as 1887 an observer, giving evidence before the Select Committee on the Butter Substitutes Bill, claimed: 'I believe that in the large towns of the North, butterine and bread is the staple food of the children of poor people.'[1] During the first decade of the present century, with butter prices rising and real wages tending to stagnate, the consumption of margarine increased rapidly to stand at nearly 8 lb per head in 1913; and in the decade preceding the outbreak of war in 1914 the Maypole Dairy increased its sales of margarine threefold.

During the course of the twentieth century a number of refinements in the manufacturing process have resulted in considerable improvements in the taste, quality and appearance of margarine. The earliest development in this direction came with the discovery at the beginning of the century, of a process which enabled the vegetable oils to be hardened in much the same way as animal fats. This discovery led to a greater use of vegetable and marine oils in the production of margarine and, as a result, to a reduction in price. The major drawback in the use of vegetable oils, however, was that, unlike animal fats, they contained no vitamins, so that margarine made from vegetable oil had much less nutritional value than that made from animal fats. It was not until the twenties that a means of overcoming this problem was found, when a method was devised which made possible the addition of vitamins A and D to vegetable-oil-based margarine without destroying either the taste or the appearance. This discovery led to the introduction of what became known as 'vitaminised margarine'. During the inter-war years a number of other improvements in the texture, smell and appearance of margarine raised it to a new peak of quality. However, before 1939 the full extent of these refinements was little realised by the majority of the population. As a result, during the twenties and thirties margarine, recognised only as a substitute for butter, suffered a serious decline in consumption as the price of butter came tumbling down from 1s 10d per pound in 1924 to less than 10d per pound in 1934. While consumption of butter soared from 14·4 lb per head in 1924 to over 25 lb per head in 1934, that of margarine declined from 12·3 lb to 7·9 lb per head over the same period, although it revived slightly during the late thirties as butter prices turned upwards once more.

Despite this setback, the British margarine industry continued to expand, and by the outbreak of the Second World War stood second only to Germany in terms of world production; the Dutch industry had suffered a sharp decline in exports as a result of the opening of a number of new factories in Britain during the thirties. During the war, with butter in short supply, margarine consumption increased dramatically and the British industry expanded rapidly. In fact, between 1945 and 1949 Britain assumed the position of the world's leading producer of margarine, and by 1950 consumption of margarine in Britain had risen to 16·7 lb her head. An increase in the butter ration in that year, however, checked the rise in consumption, and for the remainder of the fifties consumption fluctuated around 15 lb per head. By 1963 rising living standards had pushed up the consumption of butter sufficiently to cause a fall in the amount of margarine consumed to 13·3 lb per head. However, there has been nothing like the reaction against margarine as that which occurred during the inter-war years, and since the early sixties the consumption of margarine has remained surprisingly stable. This is the result of a dramatic change in attitudes towards this product. Post-war refinements, culminating in the introduction of soft-spread margarine, coupled with imaginative advertising by the leading firms in the industry, have helped to create a new image for margarine among the British public.

Although average consumption has remained fairly stationary in recent years, there has been a considerable change in the nature of the market for margarine. It is no longer associated solely with the diet of the poor, for an extensive demand has grown up among the better-off sections of the population. According to the annual report of the National Food Survey Committee for 1973, while families in income group A1 (i.e. with a gross weekly income of £85 or over) consumed 5·99 oz of butter per person each week, they also consumed some 2·44 oz of margarine per person. Families in income group B (i.e. with a gross weekly income of between £34 and £60) consumed 5·14 oz of butter per person, along with 2·96 oz of margarine each week; while in the lowest income group, D1 (i.e. gross weekly income under £19·50 with one wage earner) the respective figures for butter and margarine consumption were 4·72 oz and 3·31 oz per person each week. Clearly, therefore, although it seems that, as an item of diet, margarine is still of greatest importance in poorer households, an extensive demand now exists among households in the middle and upper income brackets, which now represent a substantial proportion of the population. This suggests that margarine, rather than being regarded simply as a substitute for butter, is nowadays seen as complementary, satisfying a specific demand in its own right.

Another of these new manufactured foods to make an important impact on the diet of the working class in Britain during the first half of the twentieth century was jam. Before the last quarter of the nineteenth century the chief means of drowning the monotonous taste of the dark wholemeal bread then consumed by the majority of the working class was to cover it with syrup or treacle—butter was too expensive and margarine had not yet made its appearance. During the 1880s, however, the introduction of a range of cheap, factory-produced jams provided a welcome addition to the diet of the working class. The considerable increase in the consumption of fruit in Britain during the later decades of the nineteenth century took the form, among the working class, of a rapid increase in the consumption of these cheap jams. Most of them, however, contained more sugar and colouring than fruit, and their nutritional value was limited. But whatever else, they were cheap (they were selling at 6d per pound around the turn of the century), and they were sweet, the two factors which ensured their popularity among the poor; consequently, consumption of these jams increased rapidly up to the outbreak of war in 1914. During the inter-war years, as sugar prices collapsed, so too did those of jam. However, despite this fall in price, consumption of jam varied only slightly around a level of 10 lb per head each year. This suggested that, since it was obviously unresponsive to changes in price, jam had by this time already become a necessity, rather than a luxury, in working-class households. Since 1945 the quality of jam has improved considerably as a result of refinements in the manufacturing process, and, as with margarine, it is now consumed by all classes alike. Average consumption, however, has shown a continuous decline during the post-war period, despite a steady decline in average prices in real terms. Clearly, jam is yet another victim of increasing affluence.

The factory production of a number of dairy products was another important development in the history of food manu-facturing, and today a considerable proportion of the dairy pro-duce we consume is made, not on a farm as we might expect, but in large, highly mechanised creameries and factories. It was the problem of transporting milk and other dairy produce over long journeys from farm to town during the nineteenth century which provided the greatest stimulus towards scientific investigation into methods of extending the shelf life of fresh dairy products. As a result of this research, before the end of the century the intro-duction of 'pasteurised' milk—sterilised by Louis Pasteur's process of heat treatment—had revolutionised the milk supply industry in Britain. By this time also, dried milk powders and tinned con-densed and evaporated milk, especially the cheaper varieties, were already an important item in the working-class diet in the United Kingdom. The factory production of butter was also well under way before the turn of the century, thanks mainly to the intro-duction of the revolutionary centrifugal cream separator, invented by Gustav de Laval in 1877. As a result, by the turn of the century, the traditional fresh Irish 'firkin' salt butter, collected from individual farms, had almost entirely given way to creamery-produced butter of good and uniform quality, for which Denmark quickly became the major supplier. As early as 1862 the Royal Agricultural Society of England's Chemical Committee granted money for research into the scientific principles of cheese-making, and eight years later the first British 'cheese factory' was opened at Longford in Derbyshire. By 1876 there were already ten such factories in operation, turning out an increasing range of char-acteristically British cheeses. In addition, during the 1880s and 1890s increasing quantities of manufactured cheeses were being imported from America and Australia, so that by the end of the century, factory-produced cheese was already a well-established item in the British diet.

At the time of the outbreak of war in 1914, however, the factory production of dairy produce was still in an embryonic stage, and it was only during the inter-war years that it began to blossom into a lucrative activity in its own right. During this period, as the purchasing power of a large section of the population increased in the wake of falling prices, the consumption of cream trebled; the major proportion of this increase came in the production of 'factory-fresh' cream. Similarly, while the consumption of cheese increased rapidly during the inter-war years, by 1938 about half of the total sales of home-produced cheese were accounted for by processed varieties. The tremendous rise in the consumption of butter which occurred during this period, particularly in the thirties, was once again largely accounted for by the growth in sales of factory-produced butter; production of butter on the farm tapered off dramatically after 1930.

Since 1945 factory-produced dairy products have continued to make considerable ground, assisted by rising living standards and the growing demand for variety in diet. Continuous scientific research has resulted in significant improvements in both the quality and purity of dairy produce. New products, such as yoghurts and cottage cheeses, have been introduced and have played an important part in the rapid growth of the dairy industry since the end of the war. The former was for centuries regarded as a crank health food; since 1945, however, as a result of vigorous promotion by the major dairy companies, it has come to be regarded as a sophisticated dessert. It was estimated that almost 100 million cartons of this product alone were consumed in 1970 in Britain. The growing popularity of cottage and other fresh cheeses in recent years stems directly from greater concern among consumers in nutritional and health aspects of food, which has tended to direct increasing demand towards fresh milk products. Paradoxically, production of these 'fresh' dairy products is nowadays almost entirely centred in factories and creameries, a twist which epitomises the transformation of attitudes in Britain during the course of the twentieth century.

One further product which gained considerable popularity in Britain during the late nineteenth and more especially during the first half of the twentieth century was custard. Custard, however, was not new to the British public in the nineteenth century, for it had been consumed for centuries in its traditional form, that is, as a mixture of eggs and milk, for purely medicinal purpose. The man who invented the product as we know it today was Alfred Bird, a chemist who had opened a little shop in Birmingham in 1837. Bird was an adventurous man who enjoyed experimental chemistry. However, it was not the pursuit of scientific knowledge

which prompted him to devise a new custard based on cornflour rather than eggs, but rather his concern to find a compromise between his wife's partiality to custard and her allergy to eggs. The product he invented was in many ways superior to traditional custard, not least in the fact that there was no longer any danger of it turning into scrambled eggs during cooking, and before long the demand for Bird's custard was rapidly outrunning his ability to produce it. To meet the steadily increasing demand he moved to larger premises in Worcester Street in Birmingham, and during the second half of the nineteenth century the business of Alfred Bird grew and prospered. With the aid of imaginative and dynamic salesmanship the name of Bird became synonymous with this new type of custard, and by the time the now traditional tri-colour designed packet was introduced in 1922 Bird's custard was already one of the nation's most popular family dessert dishes.

Of the food manufacturing industry, however, the branch which has perhaps had the most far-reaching effects on the British diet during the twentieth century is that which is concerned with preserving food. Most foods are by their very nature perishable, and in the past this has meant that they could only be eaten when in season. During the nineteenth century the growth of large urban centres, often far from the areas of food production, and the opening up of new lands in America and Australia, intensified the need for some means of preserving food to be consumed a considerable time after leaving the farm. Over the course of the last hundred years several methods have been devised to cope with this problem. During the twentieth century, however, the development of these methods of preservation has become associated not only with the ability to provide foods for consumption during all seasons of the year, but also with a specific twentieth-century style of life, in which improved living standards and increased leisure time have gone hand in hand with the dual demands for variety and convenience in diet.

Canning was the first method of food preservation to be carried out on a large-scale industrial basis, and during the course of the twentieth century the production of an ever-expanding range of canned foods has wrought a virtual revolution in the dietary habits of all classes alike in Britain.

When a foodstuff is canned it undergoes a process during

Rich man, poor man: a
contrast in diet about
1900

The works canteen, which
first appeared during the
First World War

J. D. Carr's biscuit cutting
machine, the first introduction
of mechanisation in the
industry

Modern biscuit production line

Packing special Edward VII coronation tins of chocolate, 1902

Rowntree's Clear Gums Poster, 1922

Early jam production

Butter production before the advent of mechanisation

Pea canning in operation

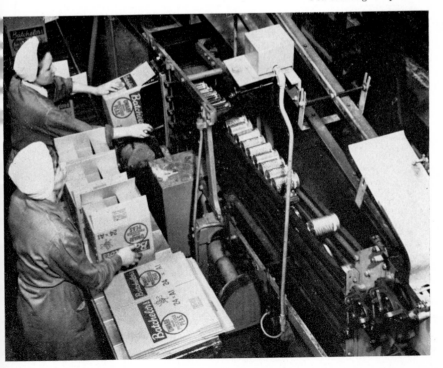

Landing Australian frozen meat from Sydney, 1881

Plate freezer, of the type invented by Clarence Birdseye

Clarence Birdseye

The first co-operative
shop, opened in Rochdale
in 1844

Arthur Brooke, founder
of Brooke Bond

Selling ice cream before the First World War

The Victorian family grocer

which it is placed in a container, usually made of a sheet of steel coated with a thin layer of tin, although glass is often used, as in the case of meat and fish pastes, for example. It is then exhausted of all air, hermetically sealed, sterilised by the application of intense heat and finally left to cool. The end-product of this process is a foodstuff in which all micro-organisms and enzymes, which might otherwise cause the food to spoil, have been destroyed, and consequently one which will remain in a perfectly edible condition for a long period of time. Nowadays, the safe lifespan of a canned food is normally regarded as being between seven and eight years in the case of meat products, and up to four in the case of fruit. However, there are no hard and fast rules; indeed, in 1938 a tin of veal and a tin of carrots, canned some 120 years before, were opened and found to be in near-perfect condition.

Although canned foods have become a major item in the diet of the British people only over the last sixty years or so, the invention of the canning process dates back to the early years of the nineteenth century. It was around that time that a Frenchman, Nicolas Appert, after several years of experimentation, discovered a new means of preserving food. His method involved the filling of the foodstuff into glass jars, standing the jars in hot water to expel air, and then hermetically sealing them with alternate layers of cork and wax. For his work Appert was in 1804 awarded a prize of 12,000 francs by Napoleon, who clearly recognised the strategic significance of such a discovery as a means of feeding his army on long marches. Around the same time an Englishman, Thomas Saddington, was engaged in work similar to Appert's, but the Society of Arts thought fit to award him only the meagre sum of six guineas, and it is in fact Appert who is generally credited with the initial discovery of the canning process. It was, however, an Englishman, Robert Durand, who first conceived the idea that tin canisters might be more suitable than bottles as containers for preserved foods. (At this time the basic metal used in the manufacture of 'tin' cans was iron, not steel.) The tin can offered a number of advantages over glass containers: it was cheaper to produce, it was lighter and easier to cut to shape, it could conduct heat better than glass, and, above all, it was more durable than the toughest of glass containers and would therefore withstand the rigours of a long journey much better.

C

With this in mind, Durand took out a patent in 1810 for the use of tin canisters for this purpose. By the early 1820s the firm of Donkin & Hall, who had bought the patent from Durand, were supplying the Admiralty with canned meats for use as ships' stores. However, apart from this and a few other ventures which followed in the 1840s, the development of canning on a commercial basis proceeded at a very slow pace until well into the twentieth century; and in fact the Admiralty continued to be the principal customer for the handful of firms which vied with each other for its contracts.

Abroad it was a different story altogether. In the United States the Civil War of the 1860s gave a great impetus to the development of canning on a large scale; and by the 1870s America was exporting huge quantities of tinned meat to Britain. By the late 1860s imports of cheap Australian tinned meat, chiefly boiled mutton, were also finding an increasing market in Britain. In the Argentine the canning of meat began on a large scale along the River Plate in 1871, and before long the name of 'Fray Bentos' was forging its place in British dietary history. However, although tinned produce was considerably cheaper than fresh butchers' meat (it was in fact about half the price), it was still unpopular among the British public. A number of food poisoning scares during the 1850s had left a great many people wary of canned foods, and in any case, much of the tinned meat at this time was fatty, coarse-grained and rather distasteful. With the development of refrigeration and the arrival of large quantities of cheap chilled meat from Australia and America, imports of tinned meat tapered off dramatically, although by the outbreak of the First World War they had revived to stand at just under 1 million cwt per year, partly because of an improvement in quality.

By this time Britain was already importing a wide range of canned foods in large quantities, for during the latter decades of the nineteenth century the canning process had been applied to fruit, milk, vegetables and fish, and huge industries had grown up in several countries, producing and exporting canned foods of all descriptions to Britain, which by the outbreak of war was already the world's largest importer of canned foods. The commercial manufacture of tinned condensed milk, for example, began in America and Switzerland during the 1850s, and within a short time Britain was importing a steadily rising amount of this product, most of the cheaper varieties of which found its way into the diet of the poorer classes as a cheap and convenient substitute for fresh milk. Fruit canning began in California in the late 1860s, and by the 1880s America was supplying Britain with tinned peaches, apricots, pears and pineapples, all of which found a ready market among the middle class. It was in California too that salmon canning was first begun on the Sacramento River in 1864, and by the late 1870s it had spread to Columbia and Alaska, where there grew up huge industries producing and exporting tinned salmon all over the world.

In the year 1880 a firm in Maine, USA, first produced what was to become perhaps the most popular of all canned foods, baked beans, or 'pork 'n' beans' as they were then known. Fifteen years later in 1895, the firm of H. J. Heinz of Pittsburgh, Pennsylvania, launched their particular recipe for baked beans in tomato sauce onto the American market. It was another ten years before Heinz introduced baked beans to Britain with a pilot sales promotion in the north of England. The response was disappointing, which is hardly surprising, since at that time few people in Britain had heard of either Heinz or baked beans. However, C. H. Hellen, the irrepressible chief of the British end of the Heinz enterprise, was undaunted by this initial setback. Some twenty years later, when the decision as to what should be produced in a new factory which Heinz had built at Harlesden had to be taken, he is reputed to have declared: 'I'm going to manufacture baked beans in England, and they're going to like it.'[2] He did, and they do. During the thirties, owing partly to dynamic advertising and partly to a steady reduction in price made possible by declining raw material and manufacturing costs, Heinz Baked Beans gained widespread popularity and became an important item in the diet of the working class in particular. It was not until 1942 that the firm of HP Ltd of Birmingham, until then known only as sauce manufacturers, began producing what was to become the most serious rival to the supremacy of the Heinz brand, HP Baked Beans.

Before the First World War, however, with the exception of condensed milk and the cheapest of tinned meats, most canned foods were beyond the reach of a large proportion of the working class. Contrary to a commonly held belief at the time, tinned salmon, at 9½d for a small tin, was never an important item in the diet of the working class in Britain. The fact is that most canned foods at this time were too expensive for most of the working class. Apart from this, those food poisoning scares of the mid-nineteenth century had left their mark, and a large section of the population still harboured misgivings about the quality of canned foods. It was not until after the First World War that increased world production and intensified competition between producers brought the prices of canned fruits and vegetables within reach of the poorer sections of the community. The war itself did much to dispel many of the doubts about the merits of canned foods, particularly among the thousands of British soldiers fighting overseas, who often depended on their ration of 'bully beef' for survival.

After the war, imports of canned foods, restricted by the war-time disruption to trade, soared dramatically. By 1924 over 2 million cwt each of canned fruits and condensed milk, over 1 million cwt of canned fish and some 700,000 cwt of canned vegetables were being imported each year. As yet, however, only a small proportion of canned foods consumed in Britain were actually produced there. In fact, in 1922 there were only three firms in Britain engaged exclusively in canning, compared with over two thousand in the United States at the time. Around the mid-twenties, however, interest in the potentialities of canning as a commercial venture intensified in Britain, and finally culminated in the formation of the National Food Canning Council in 1926, under the chairmanship of Sir Edgar Jones, a prominent figure in the Welsh tinplate industry. The objects of this body were to co-ordinate the activities of the various interests associated with the canning industry and to promote the new British industry by means of national propaganda. During the next few years the British canning industry finally began to get off the ground, largely on account of the enterprise of a handful of pioneering firms such as Smedleys, Chivers, Hartleys, etc. It was in fact Smedleys who, in 1926, introduced the first fully automatic, high-speed pea-canning plant into Britain after their chairman, S. W. Smedley, had visited the United States and had seen the great American canning industry at first hand.

Within a short time British canners were turning out the first tinned British fruits and vegetables to compete with imported varieties. Plums were the first fruit to be canned in Britain, but soon afterwards British canners were turning out a wide range of fruit in canned form, including strawberries, raspberries, loganberries, cherries, damsons and apples. Peas were, and still are, the most important vegetable to be canned in Britain, but by the early thirties all sorts of vegetables could be bought in canned form, including asparagus, carrots, beetroot, baked beans with pork, spinach, mushrooms and celery. By this time there were over eighty factories in the United Kingdom engaged in fruit and vegetable canning alone, and with prices falling steadily, especially during the worst years of the Depression, the consumption of canned foods became universal. It has been estimated that between 1920 and 1938 the consumption of canned vegetables in Britain rose from just over 1 lb per head to $9\frac{1}{2}$ lb per head, that of canned fruits from $2\frac{1}{2}$ lb to $9\frac{3}{4}$ lb per head, while the consumption of fish in tinned form doubled over the same period to stand at just under 4 lb per head in 1938. However, despite the growth of the canning industry in Britain, imported varieties of canned foods, particularly fish and fruit, continued to dominate consumption, and despite the imposition of import duties on foreign canned produce during the thirties, by 1938 Britain was still importing some five-sevenths of her requirements of canned foods; in so doing she remained the world's largest importer. Only with canned peas did British producers successfully oust their foreign competitors from their dominant position in the market during the inter-war years, and this was thanks entirely to two important discoveries made during the period.

The first related to the colour of peas and other green vegetables when canned. Peas were the first vegetable to be canned successfully in Britain, with the use of copper salts, which helped preserve their natural greenness. However, in 1925 the government banned the use of these salts in the canning of peas. The result was that all peas canned in Britain were now of a greyish-brown colour, which the public were not prepared to accept. After considerable and intensive experimentation, some food scientists working at a food preservation research centre at Campden, in Gloucestershire, came up in 1928 with a new method of preserving the greenness in peas and other vegetables; this new process saved the British canned pea industry from disaster and is in fact still generally employed today. The second, and perhaps more significant, discovery came in the winter of

1930 when a canner, while on a visit to this same food research centre, happened to notice that the researchers were using dried peas which had been rehydrated for their canning experiments. One of the major problems confronting canners in Britain at that time was that because of the seasonal nature of the canning of fruit and vegetables, canners had difficulty in maintaining production and keeping their staff employed during the off-season months of the winter. It was this problem which prompted the canner in question to produce rehydrated peas on a commercial basis, since they could be produced during the winter months; and so he began to market what he called 'Readi-Peas' and found that they were an immediate success. Within a few years all the major canning companies were turning out their own brands of what was to become the cheapest and most widely consumed of all canned vegetables, the processed pea.

Since 1945 canned foods have continued to invade the diet of all classes alike in Britain, despite strong competition from other forms of convenience food. Canners have not been slow to recognise the challenge and have responded to it by increasing the range and improving the quality of canned products already available. The biggest increases during the post-war period have been in the sales of canned soups, canned beer, soft drinks and pet foods, while a more recent innovation has been the production of complete meals, with meat and sauce in one half and rice or spaghetti in the other half of a divided 'Duo-Can'. Almost every food imaginable can now be had in tinned form, from that traditional Scottish delicacy, haggis, to such exotic items as shark's fin or bird's nest soup. As for the quality of canned foods, strict control over the whole canning process has virtually eradicated the risk of contamination and has done much to rid canned foods of the poor reputation traditionally attached to them. An example of the care taken to ensure the highest quality was the introduction in 1951 by Smedleys of a 'Tenderometer', a device to test the exact tenderness of peas entering their canneries, and so to ensure a standardised pack of the highest quality.

But the real significance of canned foods lies in the dual purpose they have served since their introduction to the British diet. On the one hand, they have removed much of the burden of preparation and cooking of food from the housewife, and on the other hand, by providing a range of foods which would normally only be available during limited periods of the year, they have added variety and, in so doing, have improved the diet of the majority of the population beyond all recognition from its state a hundred years ago. But if canned foods have played an important role in the improvement of the British diet, even more striking has been the impact, particularly in recent years, of frozen foods.

Man has been freezing food by packing it in ice for many centuries, but until the second half of the nineteenth century the practice was restricted in most parts of the world by climatic conditions, since, until that time, no method had been invented of manufacturing ice by artificial means. However, from the 1850s onwards the opening up of new sources of food supplies in America and Australia and the accompanying developments in rail and water transport gave rise to serious difficulties associated with the transportation of perishable foods over long distances such as the 13,000 miles which separate Britain from Australia. The wide price differential between English and Australian beef provided a great incentive to both buyers and sellers to find some means of overcoming the inevitability of decay in meat over journeys often lasting many weeks. Consequently, from this time dates the first really scientific investigation of the problems of preserving food by freezing. Thirty years of trial and experiment followed, aimed at perfecting a cheap and efficient ice-making machine; and finally the arrival of the s.s. *Strathleven* in London in 1880 with a cargo of beef from Australia, most of it in excellent condition, signalled the solution of the problem and the advent of a new era in the diet of the British people. Soon thousands of tons of cheap refrigerated and chilled meat were flooding onto the British market, and by the end of the century meat had become the major item in the diet of a large section of the working class.

However, the commercial freezing of food on a large scale is a truly twentieth-century phenomenon, far removed from these early efforts at refrigeration. In general, when we speak of frozen foods today, we mean 'quick-frozen' foods. Quick-freezing is the process by which a product is reduced to a certain temperature below freezing-point (usually 0°F, or −18°C) as rapidly as possible. The object of this process is to stop decay and to preserve the product in exactly the same state in which it entered the freezer. The difference between this and all previous methods which involved a slow cooling process is that, by freezing the product quickly, large ice crystals, which might destroy the cell structure of the food, do not have time to form. Quick-freezing produces smaller, rounder crystals, which reduces the danger of decomposition and enables the food to be de-frosted in a perfect condition without any nutritive loss. On a purely economic level, the acceleration of the freezing process greatly increases the capacity of the machinery, and so provides opportunities for reducing costs in the factory.

There are two methods of quick-freezing in commercial use today : one involves the use of circulating cold air; the other, the use of cold metal plates. The latter process was the invention of a now almost legendary American scientist called Clarence Birdseye. It was he who during the 1920s perfected the process by which the food to be frozen is brought into contact with intensely cold metal plates which cool it in a matter of minutes, instead of the several hours needed for traditional methods of freezing. This process was first adopted for commercial use in the United States by the firm of General Foods Inc., and within a short time quick-frozen foods had become an important factor in the American diet. In Britain, however, where people tend to be more conservative in their eating habits, quick-frozen foods took much longer to catch on. During the thirties, with the long-standing suspicion of canned foods only just finally being dispelled after a long and hard struggle by canning interests, the atmosphere was not yet ripe for such a newfangled idea as quick-frozen foods. In any case, still at an experimental stage in Britain, frozen foods were too expensive for all but the most affluent members of society. Although by the time Birds Eye frozen foods were finally launched onto the British market in 1938 several English firms, including Smedleys and Smethursts, a Grimsby firm of fish curers, were producing frozen foods on a commercial basis, the trade in these products was negligible, and it certainly had a long way to go before proving itself a viable proposition.

During the Second World War the industry ground to a halt. The government, as yet unconvinced of the merits of frozen foods, refused to allow capital to be invested in what it regarded as a 'non-essential' activity. All was not lost, however, and despite the dormant state of the trade during the war, developments were afoot behind the scenes which were to have important consequences after 1945. It was at this time that Unilever, the giant industrial combine with interests in soap, margarine and other foods, became seriously interested in the commercial potential of quick-freezing. After some painstaking negotiations, Unilever took over the company which produced Birds Eye frozen foods in Britain, and by the end of the war Birds Eye had become a Unilever brand product. Armed with the resources of such a large and powerful company, Birds Eye set out to forge a market for frozen foods in Britain, despite a great deal of scepticism from critics who believed that frozen foods were so expensive that they would remain exclusively an item of expenditure among the better-off sections of the middle class. Nevertheless, despite early difficulties associated with the supply of raw materials, the trade in frozen foods began to increase steadily. A growing number of grocers began to employ the new open-top freezing cabinets, which at this stage were being supplied by the food producers. Inside these freezers customers could find an expanding range of colourful and pleasantly designed packs of frozen foods. At first peas and herrings were the main items frozen, but the range increased dramatically during the fifties and sixties. During that time all sorts of foods came onto the market in a frozen form, including cakes, sponges, chipped potatoes and, finally, complete ready-cooked meals; these added a completely new dimension not only to domestic cooking but also to commercial catering. By 1961 there were over sixty products in the Birds Eye range alone, including meats, poultry and perhaps the most famous of all frozen products, the Fish Finger. These ready-to-cook slices of fish covered with batter or breadcrumbs were first introduced in 1955 and represented a new phase in the development of the frozen food trade, in which the convenience element was to play an increasingly important role.

Since 1945 the consumption of frozen foods has increased by leaps and bounds, defying the claims of even the most ardent sceptic. On the one hand, increasing turnover has led to reduced costs and prices, while on the other hand, rising living standards have led to an increased demand for variety in diet. Improved living standards have also enabled more people to afford refrigerators and, more recently, deep freezers; this in turn has given a great spur to the production of frozen foods. It has been estimated, for example, that in 1956 only about 8 per cent of households possessed a refrigerator. By 1962 this had already risen to 33 per cent, and by the end of 1973 over 83 per cent of households owned a fridge, although in some areas, particularly London and the Home Counties, the market for refrigerators was believed to be approaching saturation. An even more striking trend in recent years has been the steady rise in the sales of deep freezers for domestic use, in which frozen foods can be stored in relatively large quantities for months at a time, enabling the owner to enjoy considerable benefits from bulk-buying his food. The proportion of households in Britain owning a deep freezer rose from 3 per cent in 1970 to 14 per cent at the end of 1973, and the trend since then has been steadily upwards.

As a result of these developments, expenditure on frozen foods, which was a meagre £150,000 in 1946, increased to £56 million in 1961, and since then the growth has been even more remarkable. In fact, the frozen food industry represents the fastest-growing section of the market for convenience foods. Between 1970 and 1973 expenditure on frozen foods increased by over 64 per cent, compared with only 32 per cent for all convenience foods, and 32 per cent for food as a whole; and it has been estimated that if this rate of increase continues, the frozen food trade in Britain will be worth over £400 million by 1980. Indeed, as the range of frozen foods continues to expand and as techniques of quick-freezing become increasingly sophisticated, this can confidently be expected to remain the major growth area of the food industry for many years to come.

One aspect of freezing which is not usually associated with the frozen food trade *per se* is the production of ice cream. In fact, ice cream dates back to the early seventeenth century, when the Italians first produced it from ice collected in the mountains. The commercial manufacture of ice cream as we know it today, however, did not really get under way until the invention of an ice-making machine in the nineteenth century made possible for the first time the production of ice in large quantities. These mechanical means of production were first adopted and exploited in the United States where before the end of the nineteenth century ice cream had already become a popular item of diet. In Britain the manufacture of ice cream remained negligible until after the First World War; indeed, by 1920 the total output was less than a million gallons. It was during the twenties that the demand for and production of ice cream in Britain at last began to grow, albeit slowly, and by 1930, with the total output standing at just under 8 million gallons, consumption per head was already some $1\frac{1}{3}$ pints. The thirties, however, were the years of the most rapid expansion in the ice cream trade in Britain. Improved production techniques and falling prices during this period led to a great increase in consumption so that by 1939 the total output of ice cream in Britain had risen to over 35 million gallons, representing some 6 pints per head of the population.

One of the most famous pioneers in the field of ice cream manufacture in Britain was the firm of Thomas Wall & Sons. They had taken to ice cream manufacture during the early twenties as a means of compensating for the summer slackness in the demand for their principle product, sausages, and before long their novel 'stop-me-and-buy-one' tricycles had become a familiar sight on the streets of many of the major towns and cities of Britain. Another well-known name in the ice cream trade in its early days was that of J. Lyons. They also entered the business of ice cream manufacture during the inter-war years and by 1939 were turning out in the region of $3\frac{1}{2}$ million gallons each year in addition to their huge output of bread, cakes and tea.

After the Second World War, however, the demand for ice cream began to level off. Faced with what appeared to be a declining market, the larger firms such as Walls and Lyons began to concentrate their interest in ice cream of the hard type, which was already very popular in the United States and for which they thought a good market could be created in Britain. During the early sixties, however, they began to face increasing competition from a number of smaller companies who were specialising in a new product—the so-called 'soft ice cream'—the sale of which was characterised by the patrolling ice cream van complete with the familiar musical jingle. The creamy, foamlike texture of this soft ice cream (produced largely with the aid of chemical additives and air blown into the mix during the manufacturing process) made it a popular alternative to the more traditional varieties produced by the major companies, for whom it represented a serious threat. Fortunately for them, the effects of the competition from soft ice cream were offset during the sixties by a steadily increasing demand for hard ice cream in block form as more and more British households adopted the habit of eating ice cream as part of a meal. Assisted by the growth in the number of re-frigerators coming into domestic use, the consumption of ice cream in this form more than doubled in the decade preceding 1973. This upward trend encouraged a number of other food producers to enter the market with an expanding range of new and highly sophisticated ice-cream-based dessert products such as mousses and ice cream rolls etc. In this way ice cream has, over the last fifteen or so years, moved from the periphery into the mainstream of the British diet and in so doing has added a new dimension to that part of the British meal traditionally dominated by steamed puddings, semolina and rhubarb tart.

Of the other forms of preservation in commercial use today, dehydration is probably the most important. It is also probably the oldest method of preservation known to man. For centuries men have been drying meat and fish in the sun; indeed, samples of dried food over 4,000 years old are still in existence today. The principle of dehydration is simply that without water, micro-organisms, which might cause the food to spoil, are unable to grow. However, before 1945 the development of this idea along commercial lines was limited to a few vegetables, particularly peas, and soups, a stock of which Captain Cook took with him on his famous voyage around the world over two hundred years ago. The reason for the delay in the commercial development of dehydration was simply that foods dried by traditional methods tended, for the most part, to be of a very poor quality. Since the end of the war, however, several important technological develop-ments have provided dried foods with a totally new image. It was discovered, for example, that by drying foods rapidly at low temperatures a great improvement in quality resulted, and later the introduction of a new technique known as freeze-drying enabled, for the first time, a number of fragile foods, such as shrimps and prawns, to be dried intact. The result has been a phenomenal growth in the dried foods industry as the process has been applied to a rapidly expanding range of foods, including potatoes, meats, coffee, and even complete meals, all of which need no more than the addition of water and heating to the required temperature. Together, these dried products have been an addition of considerable importance to the range of con-venience foods which have come to play such a prominent role in the modern British diet.

Despite the enormous benefits which the people of Britain have derived from the development of the food manufacturing industry since the latter decades of the nineteenth century, in terms of variety, convenience, and nutritional value of the foods which now make up our diet, this development has not met with universal approval. The earliest critics of the increasing use of manufactured foods quite justifiably pointed to the deterioration which occurred in the diet of the working class during the early years of the present century as a direct result of the introduction of cheap and nutritionally inferior food substitutes such as condensed milk, margarine, roller-milled bread, and jam. However, as the food manufacturing industry expanded and the range of manufactured foods in general use widened, the claims of the critics of this trend tended to become rather more outlandish. The belief that foods produced in a factory were somehow artificial, and thus inferior to those made by traditional means, came into vogue; as a result, more and more criticism came to be directed against the composition, purity, taste, appearance, etc. of manufactured foods. Organisations such as the New Health Society and the Bread and Food Reform League campaigned vigorously throughout the first half of the present century; on the one hand, they condemned a host of alleged malpractices carried on by food manufacturers, while on the other, they nostalgically extolled the virtues of traditional foods. In addition, many individuals voiced strong opinions on the subject in the press and even in literature. For example, George Orwell, in *The Road to Wigan Pier* (1937), vehemently attacked the intrusion of so many factory-made foods into the diet of the Englishman, claiming that

In the highly mechanised countries, thanks to tinned food, cold storage, synthetic flavouring matters, etc., the palate is a dead organ. . . . Look at the factory-made, foil-wrapped cheese and 'blended' butter in any grocer's; look at the hideous rows of tins which usurp more and more of the space in any food-shop, even a dairy; look at a sixpenny Swiss roll or a twopenny ice-cream; look at the filthy by-product that people will pour down their throats under the name of beer. Wherever you look you will see some slick machine-made article triumphing over the old-fashioned article that still tastes of something other than sawdust.[3]

Since 1945, however, most complaints about manufactured foods have tended to be directed not against the products *per se*, but rather against the increasing use of chemical additives in their production. It has been estimated that food manufacturers today employ over 2,000 additives for the purpose of controlling such qualities as flavour, colour, texture and palatability, as well as for extending the 'shelf-life' of manufactured foods. Over the years the use of these additives has become an accepted and integral part of the business of food manufacture; and, indeed, it would be fair to say that without them, the modern food manufacturing industry would not exist. Some of the most ardent critics of manufactured foods would have us believe that the use of chemical additives is totally indiscriminate, and that food manufacturers are subject to no control over what they might add to our food. In fact, the reverse is the case, for, dating back to the very first Adulteration of Foods Act of 1860, a substantial body of legislation has been built up, governing the composition and sale of food in Britain. As early as 1899 a committee was appointed by the government to 'inquire into the use of preservatives and colouring matters in the preservation and colouring of food and to report whether the use of such materials or any of them, for the preservation and colouring of food, in certain quantities, is injurious to health, and if so, in what proportions does their use become injurious'. And since that time the whole question of chemical additives in food has been kept under close scrutiny, their use has been constantly regulated, and the government has not flinched from taking decisive action where it has felt there to be a danger to public health. For that reason the use of copper salts as a colour preservative was prohibited in 1925, the use of agene as a flour improver in 1955, and the use of cyclamate as an artificial sweetener in 1969.

For their part, food manufacturers are obliged to work within the widest possible safety limits when employing chemical additives. Before introducing a new flavouring or colouring agent or a new preservative, etc., a manufacturer must first submit it to long and exacting tests on animals, and, even if the animals suffer no ill-effects, the amount of the additive permitted in commercial use can be restricted to as little as one two-hundredth of that known definitely to cause no ill-effects on the test animals. Bearing this in mind, the threat to our health from chemical additives in our food appears as something of a white rabbit, and, in general, despite the claims of so-called food purists, scientific evidence consistently shows that although the greater part of our food is now produced in factories, it is purer than it has ever been, and certainly our diet is more varied and nutritionally valuable than that of our counterparts a hundred years ago.

But the development of food manufacturing has a significance which transcends purely nutritional questions, for it is clear that manufactured foods have played an important part in transforming the lives of a great section of the British population. The essence of food manufacture is that, by removing the burden of food preparation and cooking from the home to the factory, it allows more time for the pursuit of other more desirable activities. This has been an important factor in the liberation of women during the twentieth century, but it has also profoundly affected the lives of others, young and old alike, for whom the preparation of food no longer represents an arduous task. This in itself has clearly done a great deal to enhance the elements of mobility and independence in the lives of many people and, in so doing, has helped to shape the fabric of modern British society.

4

From Cornerstore to Hypermarket: The Revolution in Food Retailing

THE TRANSFORMATION which has taken place in the diet of the people of Britain since the latter decades of the nineteenth century was, as we have seen, the result of a number of concurrent developments in the conditions of demand for and supply of food following the introduction of Free Trade. The reduction of duty on several important foodstuffs; the spread of rail transportation, which opened up new areas of food production in Canada, America and Australia, and resulted in a flood of cheap imported foodstuffs into Britain; the replacement of sail by steam and its effect on freight charges; the introduction of mass-production techniques to the manufacture of food and the subsequent growth of a huge food manufacturing industry—all these combined with rising purchasing power among the working class during the last quarter of the nineteenth century to effect a dramatic and irreversible change in the nature of the British diet.

However, all these developments would have had much less lasting effect on the diet of the British working man had it not been for the simultaneous and revolutionary change which took place in the methods of food distribution in Britain. Beginning in the 1870s, the business of food retailing set out on a course of dramatic change which is still in train today and which, perhaps more than any other single factor, has helped determine the nature of the modern British diet. The basis of this change was the application of the idea and methods of mass-production to the business of selling food. The outcome, after a hundred years of development in this direction, can be seen in the 'superstores' and 'hypermarkets' which are coming to form an integral part of life in modern Britain. In order to grasp the immensity and the importance of the change which has taken place in food retailing over the past one hundred years or so, it is first necessary to go back to the middle of the nineteenth century, when the business of selling food was, as yet, a small-scale and highly skilled activity.

In the middle of the nineteenth century the constantly swelling numbers of industrial labourers crowding into the huge urban centres were already beginning to place a considerable strain on the existing system of food distribution. At that time there were three major types of retail outlet supplying the needs of the teeming masses in Britain. Firstly, there were grocers, bakers, butchers, etc., all operating from fixed premises. The grocer sold a wide range of foodstuffs which he bought from both producers and wholesalers. The baker bought his flour from the miller, and prepared, baked and sold his bread under one roof. The butcher bought livestock on the hoof, slaughtered the animals in his own slaughterhouse, and cut and sold the meat himself to his customers. All three were skilled tradesmen who served long apprenticeships to their trade. The grocer, for example, not only had to buy and sell food but also had to carry out many processing jobs, such as blending tea, roasting and grinding coffee, curing bacon, mixing herbs and spices, as well as weighing and bagging the foods he sold. Among this class of retailer, selling techniques were very different from those of today; advertisement of any kind was frowned upon, and there was no such thing as window display. Indeed, the content of the grocer's shop was usually obscured behind thick opaque glass, while inside, the food either hung from the ceiling, lay cluttering the counter or was stored away in large drawers where the customer could not see it. None of the food at this time was clearly priced. The usual practice was for the customer to haggle over the price, and there was therefore no real standard for comparison. Indeed, price competition of any sort was shunned as being unethical, for grocers were expected to acquire trade on the basis of their skill and reputation, not by underselling their competitors.

In addition, since most of these retailers carried out much of the work of processing the food themselves, the quality of food tended to vary considerably from shop to shop. Adulteration was common in all trades. For example, as the demand for white bread intensified during the first half of the nineteenth century, many bakers added alum and other substances to their flour in order to improve its colour. Milk retailers were in the habit of adding chalk to their produce for the same reason, while a favourite additive among publicans was a poisonous substance called *cocculus indicus*, which, when mixed with beer, gave it a false impression of strength and flavour. But it was in the grocery trade that the scope for adulteration was widest. The following passage, taken from the *Liverpool Mercury* and quoted in Frederick Engels' *The Condition of the Working Class in England* (1892), illustrates some of the most common malpractices among grocers :

> Salted butter is sold for fresh, the lumps being covered with a coating of fresh butter, or a pound of fresh being laid on top to taste, while the salted article is sold after this test, or the whole mass is washed and then sold as fresh. With sugar pounded rice and other cheap adulterating materials are mixed, and the whole sold at full price. The refuse of soap-boiling establishments also is mixed with other things and sold as sugar. Chicory and other cheap stuff is mixed with ground coffee and artificial coffee beans with the unground article. Cocoa is often adulterated with fine brown earth, treated with fat to render it more easily mistakeable for real cocoa. Tea is mixed with the leaves of the sloe and other refuse, or dry tea leaves are roasted on hot copper plates, so returning to the proper colour and being sold as fresh.[1]

Despite the knowledge of these and other malpractices, the working-class housewife could do little about it. Either she did not have the time to complain or she would often be too much in debt to the grocer to risk any sort of complaint. Nevertheless, the practice of adulteration did create a strong mistrust of the traditional retailer of food which, despite the introduction of anti-adulteration laws in the second half of the nineteenth century, persisted until well into the present century. G. K. Chesterton captured this feeling of antipathy in his poem 'The Song Against Grocers' when he wrote :

> God made the wicked Grocer
>   For a mystery and a sign,
> That men might shun the awful shops
>   And go to inns to dine;

Where the bacon's on the rafter
   And the wine is in the wood,
And God that made good laughter
   Has seen that they are good.

. . . . .

He sells us sands of Araby
   As sugar for cash down;
He sweeps his shop and sells the dust
   The purest salt in town,
He crams with cans of poisoned meat
   Poor subjects of the King,
And when they die by thousands
   Why, he laughs like anything.

. . . . .

The hell-instructed Grocer
   Has a temple made of tin,
And the ruin of good innkeepers
   Is loudly urged therein;
But now the sands are running out
   From sugar of a sort,
The Grocer trembles; for his time,
   Just like his weight, is short.[2]

Fortunately the shop retailer very often was not the most important supplier of food to working-class families. The grocer, in particular, tended to cater mainly for the well-to-do, and was patronised as little as possible by the less fortunate. The latter bought most of their food at the second type of retail outlet, the weekly and sometimes daily markets to which farmers and various victual dealers brought their produce for sale. In country towns these were held in the traditional market place, but in the new industrial centres they tended to occupy large indoor market halls. In these markets food prices were much more competitive than in the shops, and, in addition, customers could see what they were buying, although this in itself was no guarantee of purity. By Saturday evening, when most workers would be arriving to do their shopping, the best of the food would often have already been sold, and that which remained would usually be old and already in a state of decay. Despite this, most working people preferred to do their shopping in this way, and the weekly trip to the market on a Saturday evening became an important feature of working-class life in Victorian Britain.

Apart from the fixed-shop retailers and the markets, food could also be obtained at this time from the thousands of hawkers, pedlars and street sellers who inhabited most of the major cities and towns of Britain. The major advantage of these food-sellers, as far as the customer was concerned, was that, for the most part, the food they sold was already prepared for immediate consumption; this was an important convenience at a time when cooking facilities among the working class were generally very limited. In his study entitled *London Labour and the London Poor* (1851) Henry Mayhew described these street traders and their role in working-class diet :

> Men and women, and especially boys, purchase their meals day after day in the streets. The coffee-stall supplies a warm breakfast; shell-fish of many kinds tempt to a luncheon; hot eels or pea-soup, flanked by a potato 'all hot', serve for a dinner; and cakes and tarts, or nuts and oranges, with many varieties of pastry, confectionery and fruit, woo to indulgence in a dessert; while for supper there is a sandwich, a meat pudding or a 'trotter'.[3]

Mayhew estimated that at that time, there were some 36,000 men, women and children selling food of one kind or another on the streets of London alone. And so, by this and the other means already described, the working-class family procured its meagre share of the nation's food supply.

By the 1840s, the so-called 'hungry forties', however, it was already apparent that these methods of food distribution were incapable of meeting the demands of the ever-swelling mass of industrial labourers in the big cities of Britain. With the continuing drift of people from the land and more moving away from the centres of food production, the numbers dependent on middlemen for their supply of food rose dramatically. Before the completion of the railway network, as the distance between farm and town increased, so too did the problems of supplying the masses adequately with food of reasonable quality and at prices which they could afford. The result was that a vast section of the population living in the urban centres were forced to live at near starvation levels.

During the second half of the nineteenth century the problem of food distribution intensified. The overall growth in the population and the continuing process of urbanisation combined to produce a vastly increased demand for food in the large cities of Britain. This demand was accentuated by the fact that from the 1850s onwards the standard of living of the working class was improving and increasing real wages were beginning to produce a steady rise in working-class demand for a greater variety of foodstuffs. Among the middle class also, industrial progress brought great prosperity, and with this prosperity came a flood of new demands, particularly from those at the lower end of the income scale. On the supply side, by the 1870s imports of cheap foodstuffs were beginning to pour into Britain from several newly developing food-producing areas, and during the latter decades of the century an increasing proportion of these imports were new, manufactured food products for which there were as yet no recognised retail outlets.

Confronted with such a massive increase in the demand for and supply of food, the existing network of distribution responded as best it could. The completion of the internal railway network alleviated the problem of transporting perishable commodities over long distances, and consequently the range of fresh produce available in the large urban centres was considerably improved. At the same time the number of shops increased rapidly—faster, indeed, than the growth of population. However, in spite of these developments, the system as it existed was incapable of coping with the added burden. Small-scale retailers were unable and, indeed, often unwilling to deal with the large quantities of cheap, imported foodstuffs which were coming onto the market at an increasing pace. Their failure to equate demand and supply and to distribute adequate quantities of the imported produce to the areas of greatest need was directly responsible for the emergence of a completely new form of distribution. The principal exponents of this were Co-operative retail societies and multiple-shop retailing companies, the forerunners of the modern supermarket chain companies. The founders of these new firms, being, for the most part, themselves of working-class origin, were already in a position to appreciate the need for adequate means of food distribution in working-class areas of the large cities and towns. They saw the great potential which lay in meeting the rapidly growing demand of the urban working population of Britain out of the huge quantities of imported produce pouring into the country. As a result, the growth of these companies was based on the sale of a small number of items of mass demand at prices which all but the poorest could afford. Through large-scale buying and selling methods and by cutting out the middleman, they were able to effect massive economies, which they passed on to the consumers, who were, for the most part, the industrial working class.

Working-class Co-operative societies were the first to develop large-scale food retailing methods in Britain. The modern Co-operative movement, in fact, originated in Rochdale as early as 1844. In that year the famous 'Equitable Pioneers of Rochdale', a group of poor weavers, opened a small store in Toad Lane with a meagre initial capital outlay of £28. Incensed with the dishonest practices of traditional grocers, these pioneers decided to take the business of supplying the necessities of life into their own hands. Their aim was to buy food wholesale and sell it for cash, and to divide the profits of the business among all the members of the society at the end of the year by means of a 'dividend' on purchases. In this way they hoped to eliminate the middleman and to ensure that their members were supplied with food of the quality and in the quantity for which they paid.

The success of the Rochdale experiment in consumers' co-operation brought in its wake a proliferation of similar societies throughout the industrial areas of the north of England, and by 1863 membership of Co-operatives had risen to over 100,000. The rapid spread of the movement brought a howl of fury from 'professional' grocers, who tried in vain to disrupt the Co-operatives' trade by various methods, particularly that of persuading producers to boycott Co-operative stores. However, the policy of quality and open pricing and the idea of restoring honesty to the food retailing trade proved to be a powerful magnet against which traditional grocers could do little. As J. B. Jefferys points out in his *Retail Trading in Britain*,

The Co-operative store was practically the first store in the working-class districts of the North of England where the working-class housewife knew she would not be sold adulterated foods, would not be enticed to run up more credit than she could afford and would be told clearly the prices of the different articles. Further, it was the first store run by working men—in many instances the shop was only open in the evenings when the management committee came straight from work to serve in the store; and it was the first store that paid the profits made back to the customers.[4]

Consumers' co-operation of this sort was not, however, restricted to the working class, for the idea was also taken up in middle-class circles during the third quarter of the nineteenth century. The result was the establishment of the Civil Service Supply Association and the Army and Navy Co-operative Society in 1864. These institutions supplied the middle class with groceries and wines in much the same way that working-class Co-operatives met the needs of their members, namely, by wholesale buying and cash trading. By 1872 there were nineteen such societies in London and a few elsewhere throughout the country. However, with the advent of multiple-shop retailing, unlike the working-class Co-operative movement, these ventures tended to lapse into privately operated businesses. Nevertheless, they do serve as an illustration of the attraction of the Co-operative idea and, incidentally, as an indication of the dissatisfaction, even among the middle class, with existing forms of distribution.

The Co-operative movement proper, however, continued to grow steadily throughout the second half of the nineteenth century, and when imports of cheap foodstuffs began to arrive in Britain in large quantities the Co-operative retail societies were in the vanguard of the movement to distribute them among the industrial working class. Of the greatest importance in sealing the success of the Co-operative movement in this direction was the establishment of the Co-operative Wholesale Society in 1863 and the Scottish Co-operative Wholesale Society in 1868 as umbrella buying organisations for all the retail societies. During the last quarter of the nineteenth century these two bodies were among the first to develop the large-scale purchasing of imported foodstuffs and, later, the manufacture of food products. By the end of the century they were supplying nearly 1,500 Co-operative retail societies, mostly in the North-East and in Scotland, with a wide range of foodstuffs. By this time they were dealing directly with overseas producers and had established depots in New York, Sydney, Copenhagen, Hamburg, Montreal, Rouen and other leading centres of trade; they possessed a considerable merchant fleet and owned several tea plantations. At home they produced a wide range of groceries, including biscuits, preserves, cocoa and lard, in six factories throughout the country. And all the time the market for their products was growing. In 1900 the Co-operative movement in Britain had some 1,700,000 members and was doing business to the value of over £50 million per year. Despite the rise of other forms of retailing, the Co-operative societies continued to be the most important supplier of food to the working class in the big cities of the north of England. Loyalty to the Co-operatives, which was always strong in any case, was intensified by the fact that throughout much of the late nineteenth century most societies were paying good dividends, up to five shillings in the pound in many cases. And the growth of the Co-operative movement did not falter during the early years of the present century; indeed, when war broke out in 1914 the total membership stood at over 3 million. By this time the Co-operative retail societies were responsible for over 15 per cent of the total sales of food in the United Kingdom.

During the latter decades of the nineteenth century, however, the Co-operative movement was meeting increasing competition from a growing number of privately operated multiple-shop retailing companies also specialising in the sale of cheap, imported provisions. These firms were springing up in all the major urban centres throughout the country to cater for the rising demand of the industrial working class. As it became apparent that the existing methods of food distribution were incapable of coping with the huge volume of produce flooding in from abroad, the need for some new form of retail outlet became urgent. In this situation, the business of food retailing proved to be an area of great opportunity for a number of enterprising young men. By buying imported provisions in bulk quantities and distributing them through a network of branch shops, usually locally to begin with, but later nationally, these multiple retailers were able to achieve considerable economies of scale, which they passed on to the consumer through the medium of lower prices. The emphasis in the branch shops of the multiples was on low prices and cash transactions, accompanied by vigorous advertising, all practices which were anathema to the traditional grocer, who for the first time was confronted with the reality of price competition.

The new shops themselves were little more than shells—'food sales halls' would have been a more accurate description. The different companies each had a standardised form of decoration, and each store was given the particular firm's characteristic 'fascia'. Inside they contained no comforts or amenities; usually the only fitting was a counter. The practice was for goods to be displayed on rails hanging outside the shop or in open shop fronts. The personal attention of the traditional grocer was replaced by rapid sales of a narrow range of standardised food products. Towards the end of the century, as food manufacturing expanded, the multiples became the natural outlets for a wide range of manufactured food products. Indeed, by the turn of the century most of the major firms were actively engaged in producing these products themselves for distribution through their own and other shops.

The first firm to have more than ten retail branches in the grocery trade was the London company of Walton, Hassell & Port, which in 1870 already had thirty branches in operation in and around London. Over the next thirty years, however, the growth in the number of multiple-shop retailing companies was remarkable. By the turn of the century there were well over one hundred food retailing companies in Britain with ten or more branches, operating some 6,000 shops between them. At the outbreak of war in 1914 three firms, Home and Colonial Stores, the Maypole Dairy Company and Thomas Lipton Ltd, had over 500 branches each, and by this time the multiple retailing principle had penetrated all but the most remote parts of the country.

The traditional archetype, and perhaps the most famous of all the multiple retailers, was Thomas Lipton. It was in 1871, at the age of twenty-one, that Lipton opened his first provision shop in Stobcross Street, Glasgow. He did so with a capital outlay of only £100, the savings of four years spent working and travelling in America. Initially, he specialised in ham, bacon, eggs, butter and cheese, which he imported direct from producers in Ireland. By doing so he was able to undersell his rivals, and, as a result, his business expanded rapidly. By 1878 he had four shops in different parts of Glasgow and he was buying his stocks not only from

Ireland but also from America and Canada. Lipton's greatest asset, apart from his undoubted business acumen, was his great belief in, and flair for, advertising. While in America he had been struck by the way in which advertisement played such an important role in the selling process. He saw how American businessmen wooed their customers with finely displayed goods, with huge hoardings and full-page newspaper advertisements. Such practices were, of course, frowned upon in Britain, but Lipton decided to ignore tradition and to use his American experience to his own advantage. In the early days he used local newspapers extensively to advertise his existence and supplemented this with posters, displays and by a number of stunts. In 1877, for example, he issued special Lipton one-pound notes which bore the words : 'I promise to give on demand in any of my establishments, ham, butter and eggs as given elsewhere, to the value of one pound for fifteen shillings.' Although it landed him in court, this stunt served its purpose and proved to be a great success, especially since the claim made on the notes was fully carried out in every Lipton branch. Another famous stunt was the import for Christmas 1881 of what was supposed to be the world's largest cheese, which Lipton had hauled through the streets of Glasgow to the cheers of thousands who lined the route. By such means the name of Lipton had already become a household word in Glasgow by the end of the 1870s. In purely business terms, Lipton's belief in the power of advertising was closely related to the nature of his trade. Since he was underselling his rivals, his profit margins were lower, and it was therefore essential that his turnover should be large enough to ensure that his trade would yield a reasonable profit. Lipton believed that this could best be achieved by means of vigorous advertising.

His philosophy paid handsome dividends, judging from the rapid expansion of his business during the 1880s. Having broken out of Glasgow, he quickly established branches in other towns throughout Scotland, and then England. He opened his first shop south of the border in Leeds in 1881. After this, branches followed in all the major cities, until he finally reached London in 1888. By 1891 he had more than a hundred shops throughout the country and more than 5,000 people in his employ. However, the most far-reaching development in the business came in 1889, when Lipton entered the tea trade. As with his provision trade,

Lipton decided to buy tea direct from producers. In fact, he went even further by buying his own plantations in Ceylon and selling his own brand of tea. The result, as told in greater detail in Chapter 6, was phenomenal, and it was mainly on his tea trade that Thomas Lipton made his name, and his fortune, during the next quarter of a century. By 1898, when the firm became publicly owned, there were already over 400 shops throughout the world, over seventy of which were situated in London alone; there were several factories producing a wide range of groceries, and altogether Lipton was employing over 10,000 people.

Thomas Lipton was a classic example of the multiple retailer. Despite his own unique characteristics, his methods epitomised those of the new breed of food retailer who was prepared to provide the working class with the food they required at prices they could afford, without the frills but also without the commitments attached to business with the traditional grocer. To do this he needed to have a mass demand, to which end he was prepared to court the working-class housewife and to win her favour by means of his novel advertising campaigns.

Lipton's methods of cash sales, high and rapid turnover, and extensive advertising were adopted by all the newly emerging rival firms of multiple retailers during the last quarter of the nineteenth century. One of the most important of these rivals was the Maypole Dairy Company. The first Maypole Dairy shop was opened by George and Alfred Watson in Wolverhampton in 1887. Initially, they specialised in butter and in a new product, margarine. Over the next twelve years the business expanded throughout the Midlands and the North, and by 1898 there were already 105 Maypole branches in operation. In that year the Maypole Dairy Company merged with another firm, Medova Dairies, operated by George Jackson, a former associate of the Watson brothers. Medova Dairies had some eighty branches of its own, and so, when the two firms were incorporated as the Maypole Dairy Company, the business was already of considerable size. After the amalgamation it expanded at a remarkable rate. Specialising in only five commodities, eggs, condensed milk, tea, butter and margarine, turnover grew rapidly, and five years after incorporation the number of branches had risen to nearly 400. During the course of the next decade, as generally rising prices attracted custom to the more competitive multiple stores, the Maypole Dairy Company continued to gain an increasing share of this trade and became the major retailer of margarine in Britain, with factories and creameries of its own, both in Britain and Denmark. By the outbreak of war in 1914, with over 900 branches in operation, Maypole had already become a household word in working-class areas and had carved for itself a large niche in British dietary history.

Liptons and the Maypole Dairy were not the only big names in the new field of multiple retailing; of equal stature was the firm of Home and Colonial Stores. This company was incorporated in 1888 out of the London retailing business established some years earlier by Julius Drew and J. Musker. At its incorporation the new company was headed by William Capel Slaughter, who over the next twenty-five years was the driving force behind the rapid expansion which took place. Within two years of its inception the Home and Colonial Stores were operating 107 branches throughout the country. Like Lipton, they specialised in imported provisions, mainly tea, sugar, cheese, butter and margarine, although after 1906 many of their branches began to stock an increasing range of groceries, such as jam, cocoa, coffee, tinned milk, flour, custard and baking powder. By this time there were already well over 500 branches in operation, over 200 of which were situated in and around London. Another firm which specialised in groceries, as opposed to provisions, was the International Tea Company. This firm was one of the earliest in the field of multiple retailing and already had 200 branches by 1895. In contrast, a relative newcomer to the multiple retailing business was the Meadow Dairy Company. This was the creation of George Beale, who, having worked in the management of the Maypole Dairy Company for some years, decided to branch out on his own. In 1901 he opened a shop in Newcastle-upon-Tyne in which he sold butter, eggs, tea and sugar. From this starting-point, through the steady addition of branch shops and through a series of amalgamations with other firms, over the next decade Beale built up the trade of Meadow to such an extent that by 1914 it was among the leading multiple retailing companies in Britain, operating nearly 400 shops.

Apart from these huge national companies, there were throughout the country a number of smaller multiple retailing firms of a much more regional nature in operation before the end of the nineteenth century. Many of these smaller firms were eventually brought under the wing of one or other of the national giants, but several, including the now famous names of Sainsbury, Tesco, David Greig, etc., remained free to develop independently, and ultimately to break into the national market themselves.

By 1914 the multiple giants, with their characteristically standardised branch units, their intense competitiveness and their emphasis on advertising, had already revolutionised the system of food distribution in Britain. They were successful because they had gravitated to the areas of greatest need, the growing industrial centres, where they had found an insatiable working-class demand increasing steadily. They had striven to meet this demand by channelling the vast quantities of cheap, imported foodstuffs pouring into Britain onto the tables of working-class families; and later they had become the natural outlets for an entirely new range of manufactured food products, which began to form an increasingly important role in the British diet. The big multiple retailers were thus of paramount importance in determining the nature of the food we eat today.

As might be expected, the small-scale retailer was hard hit by the price competition and advertising of the multiple retailers. The leading organ of the traditional grocery trade, *The Grocer*, spared no effort to voice the sentiments of its subscribers throughout the latter decades of the nineteenth century. In one editorial, referring to the spread of the multiples, it declared: 'They go everywhere nowadays and even the most remote part of the country is not wholly exempt from their maleficent influence.'[5] By the early years of the present century the 'passing of the grocer', a reference to the decline of the small-scale retailer, was being sadly lamented in some circles.

However, this kind of thinking was premature, for even by 1914 many small-scale operators, by adapting their methods to cater for the new demands, were able to hold their own against the competition of larger firms. The spread of manufactured branded foods, an increasing number of which were becoming price-maintained, that is to say, the retail prices were being fixed by the manufacturers, assisted this development. All grocers, large and small alike, could stock these products without fear of being undersold by rivals, and so could be assured of fair margins of profit. Not only did small-scale grocers benefit from this, but so too did a host of traders outside the grocery trade proper, such as chemists, drapers and publicans, who began to 'dabble' in branded manufactured foods. Some indication of the buoyancy of small-scale retailing, despite the spectacular rise of the Co-operative movement and multiple retailing in the half-century or so before the First World War, can be gained from the fact that in 1914 over 70 per cent of the grocery and provisions trade in Britain was still carried out by small-scale operators. In fact, during the First World War the single-shop owner actually increased in importance. Stocking a wide range of foods, he was much less affected by food shortages and rationing than the large multiple companies who specialised in a narrow range of provisions. With the disappearance of price competition during the war, the attraction of the multiples dissolved and people were forced to remain loyal to a particular grocer in order to obtain any sort of variety in their diet.

However, when the war came to an end the march of the multiples was resumed in earnest. Competition between the major firms intensified, and the outcome was a steady growth in their size, mainly through the medium of amalgamations and take-overs. In the grocery trade, for example, during the inter-war period Home and Colonial, Maypole, Lipton and Meadow all merged to form the huge Home and Colonial group with over 3,000 branches (although each firm continued to trade under its own separate identity), while the giant International Tea Group was formed out of a series of mergers between smaller companies. In the baking trade, George Weston's Allied Bakeries grew during the thirties to dominate the national bread trade. In the meat trade, the huge Vestey concern emerged in control of over 2,000 shops throughout the country; and in the fish trade, the Unilever-owned Macfisheries rose rapidly to pre-eminence during the twenties.

Hand in hand with this growth in the size of firms went a change in the very nature of the business of food retailing. The driving force behind this change was twofold. Firstly, there was during the inter-war period a continuous shift in demand towards ready-to-eat manufactured foods. Secondly, as the practice of home cooking and home baking declined, so shopping habits changed. People tended to buy more often, but in smaller quantities, foods which were easily prepared for consumption. Despite the uneven distribution of wealth and the existence of pockets of mass unemployment, the falling prices of imported foodstuffs and raw materials meant that for a large section of the population the inter-war years brought a rise in real income. This increase in purchasing power expressed itself in a host of new demands and an increase in the amount of time and money spent on leisure activities. In conjunction with this development went a growing demand for variety in diet and the desire to cut down on the time spent in the preparation of food. In turn, this led to a steady rise in the popularity of manufactured foods, and it was this which determined to a large extent the development of the food retailing business during the inter-war period. Since most of these manu-factured foods were branded, nationally advertised and price-maintained, price competition between the big multiples tended to diminish. Instead competition between them took the form of the provision of greater service. During this period the multiples began to stock a considerably wider range of goods. They began to locate their shops on the basis of convenience and to institute deliveries to the homes of customers. In all, they began to adopt many of the practices of the traditional grocer. Ironically, during the thirties there grew up a group of 'cut-price' traders in many large towns. These men operated from unattractive premises, more often than not simply warehouses. They concentrated on sales of low-priced branded foods. In fact, they did what the multiples had done in their early days, and thereby presented a serious problem for retailers of all descriptions.

During the inter-war years the Co-operative movement, after a setback during the slump of 1921, grew continuously. By 1929 membership had increased to 6 million and by the outbreak of war in 1939 to over 8,500,000. By the latter date the movement was responsible for over 20 per cent of the total trade in groceries and provisions, over 25 per cent of the national milk trade, 15 per cent of the bread trade, and over 10 per cent of the meat trade in Britain. During this period the wholesale societies also expanded considerably. The number of food factories and work-shops operated by the English and Scottish wholesale societies increased rapidly, and their range of food products was extended to nearly all major groceries. In general, the Co-operative move-ment followed the more significant trends current in the retailing business as a whole. The shops began to stock a wider range of foods and to provide a greater degree of service. As early as 1919 the General Co-operative Survey Committee had recommended that Co-operative premises should be made more attractive by the 'opening of rooms for social and recreational purposes'.[6] Geographically too the Co-operative movement branched out from its traditional bastion in the North and in Scotland and spread into the south and west of England. This shift of location brought with it a change in the character of the Co-operative membership, for throughout the inter-war period the number of middle-class members increased rapidly and steadily. This in itself was an important factor in the determination of improved standards in Co-operative shops during this period.

Although the number of small-scale food retailers declined during the inter-war years, this branch of the trade was, none the less, characterised by its resilience. As resale price maintenance increased in importance, and as service once again became a major factor in the business of food retailing, the small shop owner found himself in a highly competitive position *vis-à-vis* the multiples. He was convenient and could stock a flexible and wide range of products. He would usually provide credit as well as a delivery service. These were all valuable assets in a period when consumers were finding less time for shopping and food preparation, and it is no surprise that by the outbreak of the Second World War in 1939 small-scale retailing was still responsible for well over half of the total trade in food in Britain. During the war once again the greatest advantage fell to those shops which carried the widest range of foods, and, as in the First World War, the competitive position of the small-scale retailer improved somewhat. However, since most of the major firms of multiple retailers had diversified considerably during the inter-war years, the improvement was not nearly so great as in the earlier period.

After 1945, and more especially after the end of food rationing in 1952, the business of food retailing experienced as dramatic a transformation as that brought about by the emergence of multiple retailing during the latter decades of the nineteenth century. The major engine of this contemporary revolution in retailing techniques was the introduction and rapid spread of the principle of self-service in food stores. The idea of self-service was imported from the United States, where it originated and where it had been in practice since long before the Second World

War. When it first arrived in Britain during the period of food control, it was regarded by many as a passing fad and as a result was approached with a certain amount of scepticism. The Co-operative movement, however, pioneered the idea, and by 1950 there were already some 600 self-service Co-operative stores in operation. When food rationing finally came to an end, there began a great rush among food retailers to switch to self-service methods, and by 1956 there were over 3,000 self-service stores throughout Britain. By this time there were already a growing number of new, larger, self-service stores, many with over 2,000 square feet of selling space. These latter were dubbed 'super-markets'. By 1962 there were almost 12,000 supermarkets and self-service stores in operation in Britain, and over the following five years this number doubled. Of this increase, the growing number of supermarkets accounted for the greatest share by far. In fact, taking the ten-year period as a whole, the number of new supermarkets grew nearly six times faster than that of self-service stores as a whole.

The growth of self-service posed serious problems for several long-established firms of multiple retailers, such as Liptons, May-pole and Meadow, now united under the banner of Home and Colonial Stores Ltd. Most of these firms' shops, having been built at a time when they were trading in a narrow range of provisions, were small (many had a total frontage of only twelve feet) and were ill-suited to the task of supplying the wide variety of goods demanded by the post-war consumer. The job of converting these shops to self-service was long and costly and occupied the atten-tion of the various companies until well into the sixties. As a result, these firms were relatively slow to enter the supermarket field, a move which necessitated reorganisation of a more fundamental nature. By 1959 the constituent firms of the Home and Colonial group had only twelve supermarkets in operation between them; however, during the sixties progress in this direction came much more rapidly, so that by 1965 the number had risen to nearly 400. But in the meantime a number of giant national super-market chains had emerged, including such firms as Fine Fare, Sainsburys and Tesco, among whom competition became fierce. The emphasis was once again on low prices. With the aid of high-powered advertising, special offers and loss leaders (goods sold at very low prices, indeed often at a loss, in order to lure

D

customers into the shop), the principle of 'cut-price' was pushed to the fore. In this way, competition became so intense that resale price maintenance collapsed and was finally prohibited by law in 1964.

Apart from their effect on food prices, supermarkets exerted considerable influence in another direction. As rising living standards produced a greater demand for variety in diet, supermarkets, on account of their size, were able to stock a wider range of goods than any previous form of food store. The use of the self-service principle, however, placed certain restrictions on the type of food which could be sold in a supermarket. The vast majority of it had to be pre-weighed, pre-packaged, of uniform quality and in standardised quantities. In addition, since goods virtually had to sell themselves, creative packaging became of the utmost importance. In all, the result was a massive increase in the production of pre-packed manufactured foods designed specifically to meet the conditions of sale in supermarkets. In this way, supermarkets were instrumental in determining which kinds of food have come to characterise the modern British diet.

Over the past decade the self-service idea has been developed to limits unimaginable thirty years ago. Huge 'superstores', with selling space in excess of 40,000 square feet, have been erected on specially selected sites on the fringes of many towns. They cater for car owners making weekly trips to stock up with frequently used foods. The aim is to enable customers to carry out this type of shopping without undue inconvenience, by concentrating a wide range of basic utility foods under one roof. The major advantage of these superstores is that their size enables them to effect considerable economies by means of large-scale buying and selling, as well as by eliminating transportation costs, since they can negotiate for deliveries to be made by manufacturers direct to the store. In recent years the idea has been taken to even greater lengths with the opening of several larger stores known as 'hypermarkets'. In general, these hypermarkets have over 50,000 square feet of selling space and can stock up to 30,000 different lines. The first hypermarket in Britain was opened in 1972 at Caerphilly in Wales by the firm of Carrefour. Since then, however, development has been slow, mainly because of difficulties in gaining planning permission from local authorities. Only a handful have been built over the past three years, although the latest to be authorised is expected to have nearly 150,000 square feet of selling space. The benefits to the consumer in terms of lower prices and efficiency in distribution are unquestionable. Recent surveys have shown that hypermarkets can undersell all rival forms of retailing by as much as 8 per cent overall, and it would appear that for this reason alone the hypermarket is certain to overcome all impediments to its growth and to emerge as the backbone of the food retailing business of the future.[7]

Despite these developments, the small-scale retailer has fared unexpectedly well. The reason is that with more people using superstores and hypermarkets for weekly 'topping-up' trips, the small, convenient shop is becoming the focus of immediate requirements. In this way, the large and small are proving to be complementary rather than competitive. The fact that one firm which controls a number of superstores is also the owner of VG Stores, a chain of small-scale grocery shops throughout the country, is evidence that large retailers at least are aware of this convergence of interests.

There is no doubt that the revolution in food retailing which began over a century ago is still in motion today. And this revolution has brought immeasurable benefits to consumers in the form of a wider range of foods and lower prices. Throughout the twentieth century the developments in retailing described in this chapter have acted as a handmaiden to dietary change, in a close cause and effect relationship. The outcome has been the transformation which has taken place in British dietary standards since the latter decades of the nineteenth century.

5

Alcohol and the British

THE CONSUMPTION of alcohol in whatever form, whether in the home or in a public house, has for many centuries satisfied the needs, be they social, medicinal or simply escapist, of men and women in Britain. Despite countless attempts to control it over the last five centuries or so, the drinking habit has survived and flourishes today. But within the last fifty years alcohol has come to play a very different role from that with which it is tradition-ally associated, and the development of this new role reflects, as much as any other indicator of social trends, the nature and extent of the changes which have taken place in the economic and social structure of Britain during the course of the twentieth century.

Since the early seventeenth century, with the exception of the West Country, where cider has always reigned supreme, beer has been the most generally consumed alcoholic beverage in Britain. Only during the notorious 'gin age' of the eighteenth century, when a tremendous growth took place in the production, both legal and illicit, and in the consumption of gin, did the possibility arise of beer being overshadowed. The intervention of the govern-ment, which had become increasingly concerned about the evil effects which gin-drinking was having on the well-being of a large section of the population, together with a sudden rise in the cost of the raw materials for gin-making, ultimately brought the gin mania to an end. Before the end of the century beer had already reasserted its premier position in the alcoholic drinks' table. Gin, however, continued to be the spirit most consumed until well into the nineteenth century, although brandy and rum were also very popular. Although widely consumed in Ireland and Scotland, whiskey was practically unknown to most English drinkers before the mid-nineteenth century. From the 1860s onwards, however, it rapidly gained in popularity and soon began to displace its rivals.

The consumption of beer rose steadily during the course of the nineteenth century, along with the increase in population, the rise of the factory system and the associated deterioration in the living conditions of the urban working class in Britain. Among this class heavy drinking became a deeply embedded feature of social life, for many working men the only means of escaping from the reality of their appalling living conditions. By 1876 the consumption of alcohol in Britain had reached an all-time peak, with each person consuming an average in that year of 34·4 gallons of beer, 1·27 gallons of spirits, an increasing amount of which was Irish whiskey, and 0·56 gallons of wine, which at that time was drunk almost exclusively by the upper classes. In the following year Professor Leone Levi estimated that, with beer selling at 1s 4d per gallon, spirits at 20s per gallon and wine at 12s per gallon, the total drink bill of the United Kingdom was a staggering £130 million. By this time the brewing industry was by far the largest of all the food industries, and the duty on alcohol was one of the most important sources of internal revenue for the government.

During the last quarter of the nineteenth century, however, the consumption of alcohol showed signs of levelling off. By the turn of the century the annual consumption per head of beer had fallen to 31·6 gallons, that of spirits, a substantial proportion of which was now accounted for by sales of Scotch whisky, to 1·12 gallons, and that of wine to 0·38 gallons (evidence that even the rich were becoming more abstemious). And this downward trend was to continue over the next sixty years, interrupted only by a temporary reversal during the Second World War. During and after the First World War, and chiefly as a result of government wartime restrictions on the sale of alcohol, the decline in consumption became precipitous. By 1930 the annual consumption per head of beer, spirits and wine had fallen to 15·7 gallons, 0·24 gallons and 0·30 gallons respectively. During the Depression of the early thirties the decline continued unabated as mass unemployment and reduced purchasing power among the unemployed curtailed expenditure on drink among the working class. A slight revival took place during the late thirties, and this gave way to a great increase in consumption during the Second World War as shortages of alternatives combined with rising incomes to produce a considerable increase in the demand for beer. This demand remained buoyant throughout the war despite widespread dissatisfaction with the continuous dilution of beer, the original gravity of which fell by an estimated 16 per cent between 1940 and 1943 as shortages of malt, hops, sugar, etc., became acute. The fact remained that the pub was one of the few means of entertainment still available and, indeed, the government, which used the duty on alcohol as one of its main sources of revenue during the war, made every effort, unlike its counterpart during the First World War, to encourage the brewing industry. After the Second World War the decline in the demand for alcohol set in once more as supplies of other goods which competed for the consumer's expenditure became increasingly available. The downward trend continued until the late fifties, when it was suddenly reversed and the consumption of alcohol turned upwards once more. This upward trend has continued ever since; although as recently as 1971, with the annual consumption per head of beer standing at around twenty-three gallons, that of spirits at over a third of a gallon and that of wine, which has shown the most dramatic increase of all alcoholic drinks over the last twenty years, at just under a gallon, the consumption of alcohol as a whole was still a long way behind the levels obtained before the First World War.

The decline in the consumption of alcohol which occurred during the first half of the twentieth century and its revival in recent years requires the closest consideration, for these divergent trends go cheek by jowl with the general course of social and economic change over the last seventy or so years. They reflect not only the changes which have been wrought in the economic, social and occupational structure of Britain over this period, but also the development of attitudes, habits and, indeed, an overall style of living which is peculiar to the twentieth century. In the development of modern British society the role of alcohol has been dramatically transformed, so much so that today the nature and extent of the drinking habit bears little relation to that of just seventy years ago. In order to obtain a clear understanding of the extent, as well as the significance, of the transformation which has taken place in British drinking habits during the present century, it is necessary to consider first of all the situation which existed at the turn of the century.

Despite some diminution in the consumption of alcohol during the latter decades of the nineteenth century, heavy drinking was still a major social problem at the turn of the century. The gravity of the situation was captured most poignantly by the American writer Jack London who, in his book *People of the Abyss* (1903), wrote:

> The English working class may be said to be soaked in beer. They are made dull and sodden by it. Their efficiency is sadly impaired, and they lose whatever imagination, invention and quickness may be theirs by right of race. It may hardly be called an acquired habit, for they are accustomed to it from their earliest infancy. Children are begotten in drunkenness, saturated in drink before they draw their first breath, born to the smell and taste of it, and brought up in the midst of it.[1]

Heavy drinking had become associated with poverty among the industrial working class since the early nineteenth century, and the revelations of Booth and Rowntree at the turn of the century provided ample evidence of the strength of the association. There was, however, at this time some disagreement as to the causal direction of the relationship between heavy drinking and poverty. On the one hand, there were those who pointed to heavy drinking as the primary cause of want in working-class homes and who therefore supported, either actively or tacitly, the efforts of the several temperance reform groups which had sprung up during the second half of the nineteenth century. Others, with perhaps a more realistic conception of the problem, viewed the existence of widespread over-indulgence in alcohol and its consequences as symptomatic of the atrocious conditions under which a vast section of the working population laboured. These conditions, it was said, forced men and women alike to seek refuge in the friendly surroundings of the public house and ultimately in the delirium of alcoholic intoxication. Whatever the relative merits of these suppositions, there could be no doubt that the existing licensing laws did little to discourage heavy drinking.

It was undoubtedly true that alcohol, much stronger than any generally available today, could be bought cheaply, beer for as little as 2d per pint in some places, whiskey for about 3d per measure, continuously from 5 a.m. to half past midnight in

London, and between the hours of 6 a.m. and 11 p.m. in other areas of the country. Only in Scotland could it be said that the hours of opening were in any way restricted : there alcohol could only be bought between the hours of 10 a.m. and 10 p.m. Undoubtedly, therefore, the opportunities existed for indulgence in heavy drinking on a large scale for those who felt the need after—or even before—a long day of heavy manual labour. Indeed, one contemporary observer recounts, in the following passage, the practice at one factory in Newcastle, opposite which stood a public house :

> This house is open exactly at six. You will find as many as 50 to 100 men all standing at the door; directly the door is opened they all rush in, and their glasses of spirits are all arranged on the counter. They toss off a glass of spirits and go straight into their work. At six o'clock in the morning, at the same moment that these men are going in, the night shift men come out, and they fill these and other houses in the neighbourhood.[2]

It was not even an uncommon practice to send out for beer and to drink it in the workshop, on the job. Under such circumstances, it is hardly surprising to find that many families were spending up to, and many more than, half of their annual income on drink. The Rev. J. W. Horsley, in his book *Prisons and Prisoners* (1898) gave numerous examples which illustrate the extent and consequences of heavy drinking among the working class. He tells, for example, of a feltmaker, earning 17s per week, and his wife earning 8s per week as a carpet bag maker, who regularly had five pints a day each and ten on Saturday and Sunday. Another case he recounts is that of a man, who spent 15s each week on drink, in prison for beating his wife, and his wife in prison for breaking the windows of a publican who continued to serve him in spite of her remonstrance. Such excesses were by no means uncommon or isolated; indeed, the statistics of convictions for drunkenness in this period reflect the widespread nature of the problem. In 1900 alone over 182,000 people in England and Wales, nearly a quarter of whom were women, were found guilty of drunkenness. This represented a staggering 51 per 10,000 of the population, compared with the figure of only 8 per 10,000 fifty years later. It should be said, however, that these statistics may not provide a totally reliable basis for comparison; drunkenness was more severely frowned upon *per se*, and was more likely to lead to arrest, during the Edwardian era than today, when it tends to produce arrests only if it is accompanied by crime. Nevertheless, the trend exhibited by the figures is unmistakeable, and the statistics themselves certainly demonstrate that heavy drinking was one of the greatest social problems of the day and that the introduction of restrictive licensing legislation was a matter of the utmost urgency.

However, despite the growing concern about the extent of heavy drinking among the working class, and despite the considerable anti-drink atmosphere generated by the temperance reform movement during the second half of the nineteenth century, there was little hope of effective restrictive action on the part of the government. Attempts to regulate the consumption of alcohol, stretching back to the time of Henry VII's statute of 1495 which enabled justices to close alehouses as part of a policy of discouraging activities 'which diverted the people from archery', all proved largely ineffectual. Most acts aimed at restricting the sale of alcohol have historically proved difficult to enforce, owing to the universality of the drinking habit and, more often than not, to the opposition of the traditionally powerful brewing interests. This power, coupled with the fact that the duty on alcohol has always provided an important source of revenue for the government, has served to make the question of drink regulation a matter of traditional controversy in the political sphere, and one avoided whenever possible by successive governments. It was Lloyd George who declared in 1915 : 'Every government that has ever touched alcohol has burnt its fingers in its lurid flames. Whenever you try to approach it there are barbed wire entanglements on every road, and passions and prejudices and principles all of the most explosive character behind them.'[3] Indeed, the fall of Gladstone's second administration in 1885, which led to one of the most important chapters in British political history, followed directly from the attempt by that government to increase the duty on beer and spirits. In the decisive vote on this issue in the House of Commons the Irish Nationalists and the Conservatives united to overthrow the Liberal regime.

By the end of the nineteenth century the division of political opinion on the subject of drink had become clearly crystallised : the Liberal Party, in keeping with its strong Nonconformist tradition, vehemently supported the efforts of the various temperance groups; the Conservative Party had become closely aligned with the interests of the brewing industry, who represented a powerful pressure group within the party. In the contemporary political climate, with the Conservative Party in power, the best that the anti-drink lobby could hope for was some form of regulatory control on the sale of alcohol, to which the Conservative government confined its activities until 1904. In that year, however, it introduced a new licensing act, popularly known as the 'Balfour Act', which immediately raised a howl of fury from the Liberal Party and, indeed, from the temperance movement as a whole. Under the provisions of this new act, the absolute discretionary power of the justices to refuse the renewal of licences without compensation, which had existed since 1552, was removed. The effect of this, claimed the Liberal critics, was to slow down the process of decline in the number of licences which had been taking place since control over the licensing of beerhouses was restored to the justices in 1869 after a lapse of nearly forty years,* and so to provide the drink trade with an unprecedented security of tenure. Coming, as it did, at the end of a twenty-five-year period during which the various temperance groups had struggled fiercely in the cause of sobriety with encouraging results, this act reflected clearly the power of the brewing interests within the Conservative Party and was bitterly opposed in parliament by the Liberals. When they returned to power in the following year the Liberals promised to introduce a new restrictive licensing bill, which duly made its appearance in 1908. This new bill quickly passed all its stages in the House of Commons; when it came before the House of Lords, however, the influence of the brewing interests was again underlined in no uncertain terms and it was heavily defeated (an event which incidentally helped to precipitate the political crisis of 1910, which led to a general election and ultimately to the reform of the House of Lords). And so, by the outbreak of the First World War, with both the major parties so divided on the issue, the opportunities for excessive drinking remained and the drink problem continued to be the major social issue of the time. This problem was to persist until the First World War, when the submergence of party differences

* Under the Beerhouse Act of 1830, beerhouse keepers had to obtain a licence, but this involved only the payment of a prescribed fee.

in the interest of national unity finally served to undermine the strength of the opposition to temperance reform.

Nevertheless, the consumption of alcohol was already beginning to decline; and if political action towards this end was noticeable by its absence, then what was responsible for this decline? There were, in fact, several forces at work in the half-century before the outbreak of war in 1914 which portended a change in attitudes towards alcohol in Britain. To begin with the most obvious, the temperance reform movement undoubtedly played an important role in creating an atmosphere in which a great many individuals began to question their need for alcohol. By the early years of the twentieth century, temperance groups such as the Christian Alliance, the Band of Hope movement, the Rechabites and the Sons of Temperance could measure their success in terms of their rapidly increasing numbers. Membership of the latter two groups, for example, soared from just under 29,000 in 1870 to over 340,000 at the turn of the century. And these groups made their impact not only among the community at large but also in the political sphere; this they did chiefly by means of vigorous campaigns against the issue of new licences in many areas throughout the country during the latter decades of the nineteenth century.

Several other factors played an increasingly important role in the decline of alcohol consumption at this time. Apart from purely economic considerations, such as the state of trade, the level of employment, fluctuations in the price of alcohol, etc.—all of which, to a greater or lesser extent, affected the overall level of alcohol consumption—it was by the early years of the twentieth century already becoming apparent that an increasing number of people were diverting their attention and money to other pursuits. In his budget speech of 1905 the Chancellor of the Exchequer, Austen Chamberlain, said : 'I think the mass of our people are beginning to find other ways of expending some portion of the time and money which previously used to be spent in the public house.'[4]

The improvement in transport facilities, particularly the railways, during the second half of the nineteenth century provided an important diversion from public-house drinking. The introduction of cheap excursions to places like Blackpool, Southend and Bournemouth, all of which expanded rapidly during the late nineteenth century, enabled many people to escape from their squalid surroundings without recourse to drink. The railway, in fact, became 'the quickest way out of the city' in all senses. Interest in sport, particularly association football, began to grow at this time and was an important factor in keeping a great many men out of the pubs for several hours on a Saturday afternoon. In the evening the music-hall, which grew rapidly in popularity towards the end of the Victorian era, and later the cinema provided serious competition to the pub as leisure-time amusements. From the late nineteenth century also, an increasing share of the income of many working-class families was being put aside for the proverbial rainy day, a fact to which the remarkable growth of savings banks, building societies and Co-operative societies readily testified. Yet another factor in the decline of alcohol consumption before the First World War was the rapid spread during the early years of the present century of cafés, such as those of the Lyons and ABC type, specialising in snacks and non-alcoholic refreshments, particularly tea, the consumption of which had been increasing steadily throughout the nineteenth century. Tobacco, too, was by the end of the nineteenth century already claiming a substantial share of the working-class income previously devoted to drink, and cigarettes had by this time already become an established item in working-class expenditure: the annual consumption per head of tobacco stood at an average of thirty ounces in 1901. The growth of multiple retailing companies, and especially of chain stores such as Woolworths, which for the first time brought a wide range of cheap household and novelty goods within easy reach of working-class housewives, provided another important means of encroachment on drink expenditure. In combination, all these factors were making significant inroads into the working man's drink budget and, in so doing, were having a noticeably salutary effect on British drinking habits.

However, before the First World War these effects were limited because of the absence of an effective licensing system, which might have accelerated the shift away from alcohol consumption by reducing the opportunities which existed for over-indulgence. The introduction of such a system under normal peacetime conditions was, as we have already observed, virtually barred by political division on the subject of drink. But the outbreak of war in 1914 destroyed the 'normal' conditions and created an atmosphere in which the Liberal government of Asquith could launch its long-awaited assault on the traditional pattern of drinking in Britain.

The outbreak of war introduced a totally new element into the drink debate, namely, the effect of heavy drinking on national efficiency and the war effort. In the words of Henry Carter, whose book *The Control of the Drink Trade* (1919) has become a classic on the subject,

> In days of peace the country had left the drinking-man to care for himself. If his health and efficiency were impaired by drinking, that was regarded as his concern; the nation took no note of the wastage, unless he thrust his intemperance on the public street and fell into the hands of the police, or drifted to destitution and came within the bounds of the Poor Law. The war drastically changed that attitude of mind. Drunkenness could no longer be treated as a venial offence. Indulgence in liquor, which fell short of visible drunkenness, was also recognised as economic loss. Its social implications became clear : the inefficiency of the drinking-man could and did delay the training or the industrial activities of a whole group. . . . Drink spelt danger; and, act by act, authority set up a fence against the peril.[5]

Against this background the government attacked the drink problem with unprecedented assurance. The first measures introduced to curb drinking applied only to the armed forces. One of the earliest regulations issued under the first Defence of the Realm Act, passed on 8 August 1914, gave power to 'the competent naval or military authority' to regulate the hours of opening of licensed premises in or around any defended harbour. Shortly afterwards another regulation gave power to the authorities to control the supply of drink to 'a member of any of His Majesty's forces'. It was not long, however, before the attack on civilian drinking began. A bill was rushed through parliament giving the licensing justices power to control, upon the recommendation of the chief officer of police in any area, the hours of sale or consumption of alcohol on licensed premises, including clubs, in that area. It became law on 31 August 1914 under the title of the Intoxicating Liquor (Temporary Restriction) Act. At the same time the government attempted to curtail consumption by raising the price of beer; in his war budget of November 1914 Lloyd George raised the duty on a barrel of beer from 7s 9d to 23s, an act which caused the price of a pint of beer to rise from 3d to 4d. This government action was accompanied by and, many thought, was a direct response to, a great propaganda campaign by the various supporters of temperance reform calling for drastic restrictions on the sale of drink. Appeals for temperance were made by such eminent men as Lord Kitchener, Lord Roberts and the Bishop of Liverpool; but none was more impressive than that of the King himself who, in the hope of setting a trend, made the supreme sacrifice of closing his wine cellars and personally 'taking the pledge'.

Following these appeals and the noble example of the sovereign, many people did in fact give up alcohol. However, at the same time a great many others, particularly women and youths working in the munitions factories, found themselves in an unprecedented situation of freedom and affluence and needed little inducement to sample the delights of alcohol for the first time. The net result was a disappointment for the temperance reformers, who saw little abatement in over-indulgence in alcohol. Indeed, the situation became so grave that Lloyd George declared in 1915: 'We are fighting Germany, Austria and Drink and, as far as I can see, the greatest of these foes is Drink.'[6]

By this time Lloyd George had decided upon a scheme which would raise the duty on spirits, beer and wine drastically and which would also establish a system of complete government control of the drink traffic in areas producing war materials. The first part of the scheme was not fully implemented, mainly because of strong opposition from the brewing interests in parliament, but the second part passed into law in June 1915 and resulted in the establishment of the Central Control Board (Liquor Traffic) to supervise and direct the organisation of the drink trade in a number of specific areas. The Board was empowered, among other things, to regulate the hours of opening of licensed premises and the conditions of sale of alcohol, to issue or revoke licences and to prohibit the sale or supply of alcohol except by the Board. Under the new regulations introduced by the Board, a drastic reduction took place in licensing hours in Britain, and during the course of the war they assumed something approaching the opening hours in practice today. For example, pubs were allowed to open for only two and a half hours at mid-day and for three hours in the evening. In London this repre-sented a reduction of fourteen hours per day on the pre-war situation and over ten in other areas. The controversial practice of 'treating' was prohibited by the Board, an action 'mainly directed at the tyrannical custom whereby members of a group of men were expected to go on drinking until each had paid for drinks all round', according to Lord D'Abernon, the chairman of the Board.[7] Another traditional practice, the 'long pull', by which a publican gave overmeasures in order to attract custom, was also prohibited under the regulations, as was the sale of alcohol on credit. The Central Control Board was also authorised to order the dilution of spirits, and under its auspices the strength of spirits was reduced during the war to 70° proof, the level which is general today. The dilution of beer followed in 1916, when food shortages necessitated the reduction in the acreage available for hops.

However, the work of the Central Control Board was not all restrictive, for, under the provisions of the act through which it was established, it did a great deal of constructive work which had far-reaching effects on traditional patterns of drinking in Britain. For example, it established industrial canteens, stimulated the sale of food on licensed premises and encouraged the sale of light beers, as well as initiating investigation into the effects of alcohol on the human body. How successful the Board actually was in reducing the national consumption of alcohol is difficult to estimate. There is no doubt that it did prevent consumption from rising, as it would undoubtedly have done, given the situa-tion in which increased incomes and greater freedom than ever before provided a great many people with the opportunity to indulge themselves. However, the greatest single factor in the drastic decline in alcohol consumption was the imposition of severe restrictions on output by the Food Controller in 1916 in an effort to combat wartime food shortages. The result of these restrictions and the regulations imposed by the Central Control Board was that the consumption of beer fell by 56 per cent, that of spirits by 55 per cent and that of wine by 34·5 per cent during the four years of war. And there was no return to pre-war levels of consumption when the hostilities finally came to an end. The restrictions on consumption during the war, combined with the new freedoms and attitudes generated by the war, helped to create a healthier and more sober environment in which drink for drink's sake was to play a lesser role in the social life of the British population during the inter-war period, a fact reflected in a steady decline in the consumption of alcohol during the twenties.

Mainly as a result of the efforts of the temperance reform groups, many of the wartime restrictions became embodied permanently in the Licensing Act of 1921. But there were other factors which operated during the twenties to assist the decline in consumption. For example, the spread of mechanisation in industry, which helped reduce the burden of heavy manual labour usually associated with heavy drinking in the nineteenth century, played a significant part in weakening the demand for beer. In addition, during the post-war period the range and popularity of counter-attractions to heavy drinking, which, as we have already observed, were beginning to make an important impact on traditional leisure-time pursuits of a large section of the population before 1914, expanded rapidly. At the same time tea and other non-alcoholic refreshments continued to gain in popularity. Under this pressure the traditional public house began to decline as a major centre of social activity in working-class areas. The growth of suburbanisation during the twenties and thirties helped remove many people from the claustrophobic living conditions which had typified the Victorian and Edwardian eras and which had provided the strongest temptation to excessive drinking. Men and women alike became more discriminating in their approach to leisure-time activity. Entertainment and food, as well as drink, were increasingly becoming the prerequisites for a night out, which more often than not meant a night spent together by men and their wives. To meet this new type of demand, the number of working men's clubs, which provided a range of facilities absent from all but a handful of pubs, expanded rapidly. From a mere 404 in 1895, the number of clubs associated to the Working Men's Club and Institute Union increased to 2,660 in 1930. The cinema—the poor man's theatre—also continued to gain in popularity throughout the inter-war period, and with two performances each evening in most cinemas, it provided a strong alternative for the pubgoer. It was estimated that by 1935 over 18 million people were attending the cinema each week in Britain.

Faced with such strong competition from other forms of leisure activity, the brewing industry set out to dispel the traditional spit-and-sawdust image of the pub and to replace it with an atmosphere more congenial to the exacting demands of increasingly fickle clients. They hoped to achieve this purpose by a combination of extensive national advertising and the improvement of public-house facilities. However, despite all their attempts to regain trade lost during the war, the decline in consumption continued, assisted by the new licensing law, the high price of beer in relation to other products and the continued practice of its dilution. During the worst years of the Depression the consumption of beer sank to an all-time low, when it was only a third of the levels obtained during the latter decades of the nineteenth century. Under the stimulus of rearmament and improving trade, and assisted by a reduction in the duty on beer, consumption of alcohol revived somewhat during the late thirties; and this revival gave way to a great upsurge during the Second World War. This fact alone suggested that the government did not regard heavy drinking as a major problem, and the contrasting attitudes of governments in the First and Second World Wars towards alcohol provides ample evidence of the remarkable change in British drinking habits during the twenty years between the two wars. As it was, during the Second World War the government gave every encouragement to the brewing industry and unashamedly used it as a major source of revenue. The number of men conscripted from the industry was comparatively few, while supplies of raw materials were constantly made available.

The Second World War, like the First, provided fertile ground for new ideas and high expectations. Wartime shortages and the increased affluence achieved by many people during the war generated a host of demands which were able to be satisfied at the ending of hostilities. In the new environment which grew out of the wartime destruction, and in the face of changing tastes and competing products, beer, which as a result of continuous dilution had attained a certain notoriety, suffered a decline in demand. This decline contributed to a general falling-off in alcohol consumption, which continued unarrested throughout the fifties; to many people it seemed perfectly compatible with rising living standards; there seemed no reason why it should not continue. During the early sixties, however, assisted initially by a reduction of the duty on alcohol in 1959, the downward trend was halted and in fact since then there has been a steady and considerable increase in the consumption of alcohol.

This revival in the demand for alcohol, it should be pointed out, has not heralded a return to the type of drinking which characterised the early years of the century. On the contrary, the revival of alcohol consumption in recent years reflects the demands of a new, affluent and discerning drinker rather than the needs of a poverty-stricken labourer. This is the real measure of the change which has taken place in Britain since the Edwardian era in patterns of drinking and in the general attitude towards drink. How this change was actually made possible is another story, involving the painful process of readjustment and adaptation of a brewing industry confronted by a declining demand for its products and a new market environment. There was little hope of a revival in the trade as it stood and the recent success of the brewing industry is due, among other things, to an increased sophistication in the methods employed by brewers in marketing their products. What they have done since the end of the Second World War is to carve a new image for drink by integrating the consumption of alcohol into the mainstream of the fast-growing leisure industry, in which entertainment and food play important roles. This trend has been made possible by the changes which have taken place in the structure of the brewing industry over the past seventy years.

By the late nineteenth century brewing was already an industry characterised by the large scale of its operations. Despite the existence of a large number of very small breweries, a handful of large firms, including Ind Coope, Watneys, Bass, Whitbread, Worthington and Guinness (which was the largest at this time), began to dominate the industry during the early years of the present century. The increased application of scientific methods which followed the publication of Louis Pasteur's *Études sur la Bière* (1876) combined with a number of important technical developments in the process of brewing to increase the advantage of the larger companies, which during the later years of the nineteenth century began to embark on a process of cut-throat competition and amalgamation to which was given the name 'the Brewers' Wars'. And this process has continued to the present day as brewers have sought to improve their market positions. With demand stagnating during most of the first half of the twentieth century, brewers could hope only to maintain their share of the market by purchasing an increasing number of smaller firms. In 1900 there were an estimated 6,447 breweries in operation in Britain. By 1973 this had fallen to a mere 163, with seven major companies—Allied Breweries, Bass Charrington, Courage, Scottish and Newcastle, Watneys, Whitbread and Guinness— accounting for over 80 per cent of the total production of beer in the country.[8] In this process of amalgamation, the acquisition of the actual breweries taken over was of much less importance to the big companies than the access to a wider market which the takeovers permitted by giving them control of a greater number of retail outlets. Under the so-called 'tied-house' system, a large brewery, following its takeover of a smaller firm, also took over the pubs owned by the smaller firm, and in this way it acquired control of these trade outlets through mortgage loans to licencees and subsequently through outright ownership of the licensed premises. Under this system, which explains why so many pubs in a specific area all sell the same brand of beer, it has been estimated that the large brewers now own over 60 per cent of all the pubs in Britain. Bass Charrington owns well over 9,000 alone, Allied Breweries owns 8,000, Whitbread, 8,500, Courage and Watneys, 6,000 each, and Scottish and Newcastle, 1,700. Guinness is the only exception, owning no pubs at all, but relying on good advertising and a ready access to the market through licence agreements with the major brewers and through free trade outlets.

Alongside this trend towards greater consolidation in the industry came an awareness among the big brewers that a change was taking place in the nature of the market for alcohol. They first realised during the inter-war period that if the decline in beer consumption was to be halted, they must cater for the demands of an increasingly discerning clientele. They therefore extended their operations into the new suburbs, building new pubs and re-building old ones and providing better amenities in them to compete with those in the increasing number of clubs. Faced with a lower output of a product inferior to that which they were selling before the war, and with high prices forced upon them by an alcohol duty increased several times during the twenties, brewers also began to place greater emphasis, both collectively and individually, on advertising. Most of the advertising was at this time centred around a range of new bottled beers on which the brewers hoped to base their revival. A 'Beer is Best' campaign was launched during the thirties by the Brewers' Society, and this slogan soon ranked alongside the by now familiar catchphrases such as 'Guinness is Good for You' and 'We Want Watneys'. All this effort was rewarded to some extent when the decline in consumption at last appeared to have been arrested during the late thirties, and the experience of the wartime demand for beer did nothing to alter this belief. The resumption of the downward trend in alcohol consumption, however, after the war shattered the hopes of the brewers, and as a result the pace of amalgamation hotted up as the big companies fought tooth and nail to maintain their respective shares of the contracting market. Before long the brewing industry was rapidly beginning to assume the form it has today.

The changes in fortunes which these post-war developments within the brewing industry have brought about have been remarkable. Within the last fifteen years a slowly declining consumption has been turned into a steady increase and brewing has once more become a highly profitable industry. Rising living standards, increased leisure time and an ever-widening circle of consumers, encompassing more young people, more women and an increasing number of middle-class drinkers, have provided a context in which brewers have set about reviving their flagging trade. Sophisticated new public houses and old ones re-vamped along modern lines have formed the backbone of the recovery. Entertainment and food have been pushed hard and the old spit-and-sawdust associations of the pub have been kicked out of the door. Drinking has become a respectable social activity.

During the sixties new products were introduced and given the hard-sell treatment, with wide coverage in the press and on television. The most important of these new products was 'keg beer', which first made its appearance during the late fifties. Keg is draught beer infused with carbon dioxide and served under pressure, a method which gives it many of the characteristics of bottled beer. From the brewers' point of view, keg beer has several advantages over traditional beers. In the first place, it is cheaper to produce and transport, but because of the novelty of the idea and with the aid of extensive advertising, it can be sold as a premium beer at a premium price. The progress of keg beer since its introduction has been remarkable. In the decade up to 1973 sales increased fourfold and by this date it already accounted for some 20 per cent of all beer sales, compared with only one per cent in 1959.

Lager, in draught and bottled form, is another recent addition to the profit-making armoury of the big brewers. Originally an import from the continent, lager has grown in popularity largely because of the appeal of its clear, light appearance and its tangy flavour and because of the reputation for high quality earned by the leading imported varieties. Brewers in Britain have to some extent traded on this reputation and on the novelty of the product to forge a market for their own varieties, at first among women and young people, but more recently, through extensive advertising, to all classes of drinkers. Lager is today the fastest-growing product of the brewing industry, and its share of the market increased to over 10 per cent in 1973, compared with only 2 per cent in 1959.

Apart from beer, the big brewers have also managed to revive sales of spirits, but the most impressive increase in recent years has come in the sale of wine. Assisted by the proliferation of plush wine bars and by the extension of retail outlets for wine through an increase of over 5,000 off-licences during the sixties and the introduction of off-licence sections by a number of large supermarket chains throughout the country, sales of wine almost doubled during the sixties. This, perhaps more than anything else, reflects the great increase in living standards and the changing tastes and drinking habits of a large section of the British population since the end of the Second World War.

However, the changes which have taken place in the drink trade since 1945 have not met with universal approval. Despite the claims of the brewers that the changes have been in direct response to shifts in tastes and demands, a considerable minority of drinkers in recent years have voiced loud complaints about the unashamed manner in which the big brewers have deliberately set out to destroy the traditional pattern of drinking in Britain. Pub closures in rural areas, the replacement of long-established tenants by salaried managers, the dilution of beer, the redesigning and subsequent reorientation of the trade of established pubs to cater for a younger, more affluent clientele, are just some of the practices decried by the opponents of the big brewers. The working man, who was for decades the brewers' basic support, has, according to the critics, been forsaken for this new type of customer. Public bars are fast disappearing as the brewers cater for an increasing number of middle-class drinkers who are prepared to spend more on a night out but who in return expect more for their money. Keg beer has come in for some of the strongest criticism from the traditionalists. They object to having what they regard as an expensive and inferior product thrust upon them through the brewers' hold on the majority of retail outlets. And their objections have prompted the formation of two organisations, the Society for the Preservation of Beers from the Wood, formed in 1963, and the more recent and more militant Campaign for Real Ale, to press their claims through the media and in parliament and to advise their members of the whereabouts of pubs selling traditional draught beer, brewed by a dwindling number of independent brewers. Membership of these two groups has grown considerably over the past few years, and with several MPs taking up the cause of consumer protection, a certain amount of political pressure is now being brought to bear in parliament. An interesting offshoot of the growing dissatisfaction among many drinkers is the great increase which has taken place in recent years in the practice of home brewing. During the last five years a number of companies have grown up, supplying kits for making beer and wine in the home, and it has been estimated that over half a million people now brew their own beer and drink it at home.

However, despite the protests of those who yearn for a return to the good old days when a man could go to the pub for a quiet pint and a game of darts or cribbage with his friends, the fact remains that for the majority of the drinking population today increased affluence has raised expectations and created new demands and, in so doing, has helped to develop an attitude towards drink which is incompatible with the old image of the pub. For example, in a survey carried out in 1970 by the Office of Censuses and Surveys into public attitudes to the licensing law, it was reported that 64 per cent of the informants, when asked about their idea of a pub, agreed that they would prefer somewhere where the whole family could be together, a figure which underlines the trend away from the pub as the sole sphere of the man of the house. Furthermore, in recommending that future licensing laws should allow for the development of social trends, the Erroll Report on Liquor Licensing stated in 1972 that 'For the vast majority of people alcohol is used not primarily as a drug from which to obtain artificial stimulus, but as a social solvent, enjoyed as much for its taste as for its relaxing qualities and that in the vast majority of cases it is incidental to some wider social purpose.'[19] In this statement lies the true extent of the change which has taken place, not only in British drinking habits, but also in the whole pattern of social and economic life during the course of the twentieth century.

6

The Cups that Cheer: The Rise of the Non-alcoholic Beverage

THE TRENDS in alcohol consumption over the past hundred years or so, described in the previous chapter, were indicative of a more general change taking place in traditional British drinking habits. However, these trends were themselves influenced to a great extent by a number of developments taking place over the same period, which resulted in a tremendous increase in the supply and consumption of several non-alcoholic beverages. The rapid growth in the popularity of these beverages since the latter decades of the nineteenth century has had a profound effect on attitudes in Britain towards alcohol, and their existence as real alternatives to beer and spirits has played a significant role in determining the levels of alcohol consumption during the twentieth century.

By far the most important of these non-alcoholic drinks is tea. During the last quarter of the nineteenth century, under the stimulus of a number of favourable circumstances, this product became what it remains today, the universal drink of all classes alike in Britain—a fact which has earned the country the reputation of being a nation of tea-drinkers. However, as with most items of our diet which we now tend to take for granted, tea was for many years after its introduction to England in the middle of the seventeenth century an expensive luxury, consumed (in Chinese style without milk or sugar) exclusively by the upper classes. When Samuel Pepys sent in 1660 'for a cup of tee (a China drink) of which I have never drunk before', it was selling for between £3 and £4 per pound, and despite several reductions in price over the next forty years, tea remained confined to the tables of the rich. During the course of the eighteenth century, however, the price continued to fall as imports of tea, almost entirely from China, expanded rapidly from around 2,000 lb in 1700 to nearly 20 million lb per year by the end of the century. As a result, the popularity of tea became more widespread and its consumption increased considerably to stand at nearly $1\frac{1}{2}$ lb per head per year at the end of the century.

Among the middle class the consumption of tea became highly fashionable. Indeed, Dr Johnson proudly described himself as 'a hardened and shameless tea-drinker, who has for twenty years diluted his meals with only the infusion of the fascinating plant, whose kettle has scarcely time to cool; who with tea amuses the evening, with tea solaces the midnight, and with tea welcomes the morning'.[1] More significant was the fact, reported by Sir Frederick Eden in 1797, that tea in small quantities was already a common feature in the diet of labourers in the south of England, and it was from there, during the course of the next fifty years, that the consumption of tea spread among the working class throughout the country. During this time the consumption per head varied between 1 lb and $1\frac{1}{2}$ lb per year. But with the population increasing rapidly, the actual amount of tea consumed in Britain during the first half of the nineteenth century more than doubled.

An important boost was given to the consumption of tea in 1833, when the monopoly of the Chinese tea trade, held by the East India Company since the seventeenth century, was finally brought to an end. With the demise of the East India Company came an end to import restrictions and artificially maintained prices. The major obstacle now remaining to the rapid growth of tea consumption was the government duty on imported tea. Before the advent of Free Trade the government regarded the trade in tea as a good source of revenue, and although the actual cost of the cheapest varieties of tea had fallen to around 10d per pound by the middle of the nineteenth century, the duty raised this to 3s per pound in the shops. Nevertheless, by the 1840s tea had already become such an important item in the diet of the working class throughout the country that Frederick Engels, describing in 1844 the average diet of the working class in Manchester as consisting of variable quantities of bread, potatoes, bacon and cheese, could report that 'As an accompaniment, weak tea, with perhaps a little sugar, milk or spirits is universally consumed. Tea is regarded in England and even in Ireland as quite as indispensable as coffee in Germany, and where no tea is used the bitterest poverty reigns.'[2]

During the second half of the nineteenth century, however, the consumption of tea increased at an even more remarkable rate; it was during this period that tea established its position as the national drink, consumed by all classes alike. Two sets of circumstances combined to bring about this situation. In the first instance, increased taxation, the introduction of restrictive licensing on alcohol and the new standards of respectability set by the success of the temperance reform movement were beginning to have an adverse effect on the level of alcohol consumption in Britain during the last quarter of the nineteenth century; over the same period, a series of reductions in the tea duty were having the opposite effect on the consumption of tea, as falling prices served for many people to make tea a more attractive alternative to beer than ever before. In the second place, the opening up of new sources of tea supply in India and later Ceylon, and the entry into the tea trade of several giant multiple retailing companies, the first and by far the most important of which was Thomas Lipton & Co., led to an inflow of massive quantities of tea to Britain, which produced further reductions in price as well as a significant improvement in the general standard of quality.

In 1840 the duty on tea stood at 2s 6d per pound. In 1853 Gladstone began a gradual process of reduction by cutting the duty to 1s 10d. By 1863 it had been reduced to 1s, and by the turn of the century it had fallen to 5d. The result was that while the consumption of beer began to falter after reaching a peak in 1876, the consumption of tea surged ahead and by the turn of the century it had risen to over 6 lb per head and, as the dietary surveys of Booth and Rowntree readily testify, it had become an indispensable part of working-class diet. However, the culmination of the progress of tea-drinking in Britain came in 1894 with the opening of the first Lyons' tea shop at 213 Piccadilly in London. The success of this and the fifteen shops which followed within the next year demonstrated clearly that tea at last reigned supreme amongst non-alcoholic beverages.

During the second half of the nineteenth century tea had, of course, become the most powerful weapon in the armoury of the temperance reformers—'the cups that cheer but not inebriate'. And it was Gladstone himself who declared in his budget speech of 1882 : 'The domestic use of tea is a powerful champion able to encounter alcoholic drink in a fair field and throw it in a fair fight.'³ Indeed, such was the attraction of tea that a great many people in Britain forsook alcohol altogether in its favour during the later decades of the nineteenth century. Joseph Rowntree and Arthur Sherwell estimated that by the end of the century there were already over 3 million adult teetotallers in the United Kingdom, with the numbers increasing every day.

That the consumption of tea was able to rise so rapidly during the second half of the nineteenth century can largely be explained by the growth of production in India and Ceylon. Until the 1870s China was the major source of the tea supply of Britain, providing some 85 per cent of all tea imports into the country; and the famous races between the old tea clippers on the Chinese route provided a source of intense interest and excitement captured in the press of the day. In the second half of the nineteenth century, however, under the initiative of the Governor-General of India, Lord William Bentinck, the possibilities of growing tea on a commercial scale in India were explored. The success of the initial ventures quickly gave rise to a rapid expansion in the area under cultivation. As a result, by the 1870s there was already a brisk trade of some 40 million pounds of tea each year between India and Britain, and the Chinese trade rapidly lost ground. The success of the tea industry in India, and later Ceylon, was largely due to the fact that the tea produced in these countries was cheaper and of a more uniform quality than the Chinese varieties. This stemmed from the differences in production methods between the two. In India and Ceylon tea was a plantation crop, readily controlled and supervised for quality and marketed under a much more efficient management than China tea, which was grown by myriads of small producers and sent to market in widely differing conditions. The application of steamship and rail to the transportation of Indian tea compounded the already significant cost advantage over the Chinese varieties, so that before the end of the 1880s Indian tea dominated the British market.

It was at this time that a series of events occurred which were responsible for bringing about a transformation in the nature of the tea trade, which as a result became characterised by the sale of tea of a high and uniform quality at very low prices. The instrument of this transformation was the entry of Thomas Lipton into the tea trade in 1889. In that year Lipton visited Ceylon and bought five tea plantations. He had conceived the idea that by cutting out the middlemen in the tea trade—the wholesalers and brokers of Mincing Lane in London, the headquarters of the British tea trade—he could sell his own tea much more cheaply than anyone else. Furthermore, he determined to sell his tea in standardised packets bearing his brand name. At that time only a small proportion of tea was sold in this way, the usual practice being for retailers to store the tea in chests and weigh out individual amounts for customers as required, a method which encouraged many grocers to adulterate their tea and to sell underweight. Under the slogan 'Direct from the Garden to the Teapot', Lipton began to retail his own tea in one-pound, half-pound and quarter-pound packets at prices ranging between 1s 2d and 1s 9d per pound, which compared with average prices in family grocers ranging between 3s and 4s. In so doing, he effected a virtual revolution in the tea trade in Britain as other multiple retailing companies were forced to follow suit. Thomas Lipton's entry into the tea trade made him a multi-millionaire within a few years, but more significantly, it also secured the position of tea as the single most important beverage in the British diet.

Throughout the early decades of the twentieth century the consumption of tea rose steadily. During the First World War, along with war bread and margarine, 'government control tea' became one of the mainstays of the British diet, and after 1918 the ending of food control and the reintroduction of the major proprietary brands saw a further increase in the levels of consumption. By 1935 every man, woman and child in Britain was drinking an estimated 10 lb of tea each year, representing an overall consumption of 200,000 tons compared with around 75,000 tons fifty years earlier. During this period it was the Co-operative Wholesale Society which became the giant of the tea trade. By the thirties the Society was responsible for some 30 per cent of the tea market. However, its dominance of the market was soon to be challenged and ultimately undermined by the rise of the best-known of all the tea suppliers this century, Brooke Bond.

In 1869, twenty years before Thomas Lipton made his momentous voyage to Ceylon, a young man called Arthur Brooke opened a small shop at 29 Market Street, Manchester for the sale of tea, coffee and sugar only. The nameplate above this shop read 'Brooke Bond & Co., Limited'. In actual fact there was no Mr Bond; the name appeared because Brooke thought it sounded well. From these humble beginnings the business of Arthur Brooke flourished, and during the course of the twentieth century it grew into a huge world-wide venture, with plantations in India, Pakistan, Ceylon and Africa and associated companies in Europe, the United States and Canada. In Britain Brooke Bond became a household word as the famous 'Dividend' range, launched in 1935, and PG Tips, also launched during the thirties, came to dominate the British tea market. By the outbreak of war in 1939, Brooke Bond was already one of the top four leading tea suppliers in Britain. After the Second World War and the decontrol of the tea trade in 1952, Brooke Bond quickly forged ahead of its rivals. Extensive and creative advertising, the best-known example of which featured the now famous Brooke Bond chimps, helped to boost Brooke Bond's share of the market. By the mid-sixties, with PG Tips and Triple Divi both clear market leaders, Brooke Bond was responsible for around 30 per cent of the total sales of tea in Britain.

The market was, however, a declining one, for even before the outbreak of war in 1939 there were signs that the scope for further increase in the level of tea consumption was limited as the demand for tea began to falter and even decline slightly. This seems hardly surprising since, on the assumption that one pound of tea will make in the region of 190 cups, the average consumption figure of 10 lb per year achieved during the mid-thirties implies an average daily consumption of five cups of tea at that time. This in itself suggested that the market for tea was already approaching saturation point. Other factors were also coming into operation at this time which affected the level of tea consumption. Recovery from the Depression brought with it a rise in purchasing power for a large section of the population, and the demand for an increasing range of new consumer goods was already beginning to make inroads into the demand for such basic staples of diet as tea. The arrival of war, however, prevented the decline in tea consumption from reaching measurable proportions. With food supplies limited by the wartime dislocation of trade, tea played a vital part in filling the gap left by the disappearance of many foods from the British diet. Indeed, the official history of the Second World War records that 'People couldn't run a village dance, raise money for Spitfire funds, get married or maintain morale in air raids without tea.'[4]

However, after the interruption of the Second World War and after the end of government control in 1952, the downward trend in the consumption of tea was resumed in earnest. Rising living standards among the majority of the population created a host of new demands and resulted in a new diversity in diet which struck at the very roots of the demand for such staples as bread and tea. By 1968, with the consumption per head of the population standing at nearly $8\frac{1}{2}$ lb, tea accounted for 62 per cent of the total expenditure on non-alcoholic beverages in Britain, compared with 71 per cent five years earlier, and this took place despite a decline in the price of tea, in real terms, over the same period, of over 20 per cent. By 1973 the share of tea in the total expenditure on non-alcoholic beverages had fallen further to just over 50 per cent, by which time the consumption per head stood at 7 lb. Over this same period the consumption of coffee and alcohol increased rapidly, despite rising prices. This suggests that the consumption of tea is no longer responsive to changes in its price, a fact which signifies that an important shift in consumer preference away from tea has taken place since the end of the Second World War.

In an attempt to stem the tide, the Tea Council during the sixties initiated a programme of national advertising, the basis of which was the familiar 'Join the Tea Set' slogan. At the same time the tea supply companies, in an attempt to create a new image for tea, introduced the tea bag, which quickly gained widespread popularity and a sizeable share of the market. Neither scheme could, however, stem the overall decline in tea consumption, which suggests that the shift in demand was of a more fundamental nature. This shift reflects the immense changes which have taken place in the nature of the economy and society of Britain during the course of the twentieth century. It reveals the gulf in living standards which separates us from our Victorian counterparts and provides a measure of the extent to which Britain has cast off its nineteenth-century mantle, characterised by a working-class diet in which tea was a central and indispensable element. As with bread, the basic necessity of yesterday has become today an adjunct of choice.

The most serious challenge to the supremacy of tea as the

national drink in Britain has come from the rapid growth since 1945 in the consumption of coffee, particularly the instant varieties. Coffee, however, is not by any means a recent innovation, for its meteoric rise in popularity in recent years was preceded by over three hundred years during which it occupied a relatively minor role in the national diet.

Coffee, in fact, first came to Britain, along with tea and chocolate, around the middle of the seventeenth century, and its immediate popularity among the upper classes soon gave birth to a number of establishments known as coffee-houses. These coffee-houses, the first of which was opened in 1652, in St Michael's Alley in London, became renowned as meeting places where men could smoke, read, engage in discussion and even conduct business. Indeed, it was in a coffee-house owned by him that a certain Mr Lloyd, the founder of the world-famous London insurance agency of that name, originally carried out his transactions. During the course of the eighteenth century, however, as tea became cheaper and more freely available, coffee began to lose ground, and before the end of the century many of the once famous London coffee-houses had disappeared. By 1801, when the consumption per head of tea had risen to nearly 1½ lb, that of coffee had fallen to a mere one ounce. This trend was curbed during the next fifty years, when the duty on coffee was reduced several times, resulting in a considerable revival in consumption. In 1824, for example, the duty was cut from 1s to 6d, and by 1841 the consumption per head had risen to nearly 1½ lb. The duty was further reduced to 4d in 1842, and by 1845 consumption per head had risen to just under 2 lb.

At this time coffee was still essentially a drink for the middle class and, unlike tea, it was rarely found in the diet of working-class families. But there was an increasing number of street stalls selling coffee in London at this time. Henry Mayhew reported that the number of these coffee-stalls had increased since the 1820s, not only as a result of the fall in the price of coffee which followed the cuts in duty, but also because of the facility with which the coffee-sellers could and did adulterate their coffee with ground chicory, which was in turn often adulterated with baked carrots and saccharine roots. According to Mayhew, there were some 300 of these coffee-stalls in 1842, selling between them over 550,000 gallons of coffee annually in the streets of London.

When Gladstone reduced the duty on imported coffee to 3d in 1853, the scene appeared to be set for a great upsurge in the consumption of coffee, and, indeed, between 1850 and 1880 the consumption more than doubled. However, the opening up of new sources of tea supply in India and Ceylon and the entry of the giant multiple retailers into the tea trade sealed the fate of coffee over the next sixty years or so. As tea rapidly asserted its position as the national drink, the popularity of coffee began to wane; already by 1890 consumption per head had fallen to ¾ lb, and it remained virtually stationary at this level until the late thirties. By the inter-war period the consumption of coffee was only about 10 per cent by weight of tea consumption. In 1930, for example, with consumption per head at just over ¾ lb, the total consumption of coffee in Britain barely touched 20,000 tons.

Furthermore, even by this time, coffee still retained its traditional class associations. For example, in a dietary survey carried out by Sir William Crawford during the thirties, it was revealed that the consumption of coffee as a breakfast drink as between different income groups represented in the sample was as shown in Table 5. Clearly coffee was still a staunchly middle- and upper-

Table 5

Consumption of coffee by income group in the 1930s

Class	AA	A	B	C	D
Income	£1,000+	£500–999	£250–499	£125–249	under £125
Percentage using coffee	43·4	17·6	8·1	2·2	1·2

class drink. This was the case simply because coffee was still much more expensive than tea. Apart from the actual price differences between the two, which fluctuated between 1d and 8d per pound during the inter-war period, the amount of liquid which could be produced from one pound of coffee at the time was only about a quarter of that which could be produced from one pound of tea.

Coffee-stall in London, about 1900

The muffin man, about 1870

Thomas Lipton

Maypole Dairy shop, Liverpool, 1902

Carrefour hypermarket, Eastleigh

Cheap fish stall, 1877

'The Pious Public House': *Punch* cartoon, 1860, captioned: 'A place in which the great brewers don't see any particular harm'

An ultra modern pub: interior of Ind Coope's 'Horseshoe', Tottenham Court Road, London's biggest pub

Guinness advertisement

Skol lager brewery: a view of the brewhouse, Alloa, Scotland

Packing tea by hand before the advent of mechanisation

Lyons' first teashop, 213 Piccadilly, London, 1894

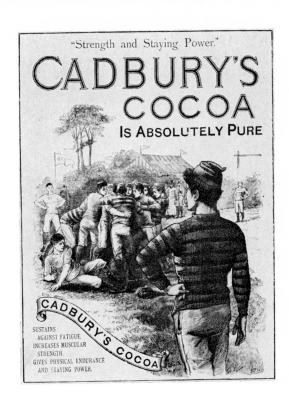

Advertising cocoa, 1888

The most famous of the early Bovril advertisements, which first appeared as a poster in 1896

London milkman, 1920, with both tapped milk, from which customers filled their own cans, and the more recently introduced bottled milk

Saturday night out, 1951 – drinking soda po

For that reason, coffee held little attraction for a working class ravaged by unemployment.

Towards the late thirties, however, with the consumption of tea beginning to show signs of levelling off in the wake of economic recovery, that of coffee revived slightly. After the Second World War, during which the dislocation of trade caused the import of raw coffee to be severely curtailed, the revival in the consumption of coffee became pronounced. Rising living standards and the accompanying demands for variety in diet began to override economic considerations in the choice of food, and although coffee remained relatively more expensive than tea, the latter began to lose ground as public taste, more than ever subjected to American influence, came increasingly to favour coffee. By 1963 the consumption of coffee was nearly three times greater than before the war, with coffee now accounting for 21 per cent of the total sales of non-alcoholic beverages. By 1968 this share had increased to 30 per cent, and in 1973 it stood at over 40 per cent, by which time every man, woman and child in Britain was consuming an annual average of almost 2 lb of coffee.

If one single explanation were sought for this dramatic shift in consumer preference away from tea to coffee, the development of 'instant' coffee would provide as good an answer as any. Before the introduction of instant coffee in 1938, the lengthy process of grinding and roasting required to make coffee was a strong factor militating against the spread of its use. Various different forms of coffee (for example, liquid extracts and crystals) had appeared on the market during the inter-war years, but none of them made any real impact, since most were not completely soluble, nor did they taste or smell like freshly ground coffee. It was in 1930 that the Nestlé Company of Switzerland first began investigations into the idea of producing a ready-prepared coffee. Their interest stemmed from an approach made to them by a group of Brazilian coffee-growers who were in financial difficulties as a result of persistent overproduction. These men were anxious to increase the consumption of coffee throughout the world and felt that a coffee which could be produced and sold in conveniently standardised packets would provide the answer to their problems. It was 1937, however, before Nestlés finally overcame the problem of preserving the flavour and aroma of the coffee: this they achieved by the addition of carbohydrates. In the following year

E

they finally launched their new product, which took the form of a soluble powder, not cubes as had originally been suggested. The name of the new product, a household word today, was Nescafé, the manufacture of which began in England in 1939.

Unfortunately, the Second World War robbed Nestlés of the benefits which they were sure to have gained from being first in the market with the new product. With patent regulations becoming relaxed, and with production of Nescafé curtailed by shortages of raw coffee, the war provided a breathing space in which Nestlés' competitors were able to develop their own brands of instant coffee. The result was that when rationing finally came to an end, Nescafé had several rivals. A vigorous price war ensued which, although detrimental to the companies involved at the time, ensured the future of instant coffee in the diet of all classes alike in Britain. It was 1954 before the greatest rival to Nescafé, Maxwell House, first appeared on the British market. Extensive advertising, particularly through the medium of the new commercial television network, quickly made Maxwell House a reputable brand name, and by 1960 it accounted for over 20 per cent of the market for instant coffee, which by this time was already worth some £16 million. Between 1960 and 1973, as the value of instant coffee sales rose to nearly £60 million, the consumption of instant coffee more than trebled from 0·14 oz to 0·47 oz per person per week, and by the latter date it already accounted for over two-thirds of the total consumption of coffee. The application of the freeze-drying process to coffee in recent years and the production of granular coffee, which has led to a great improvement in quality by increasing the resemblance of instant to freshly ground coffee, have been important factors in the rapid growth of coffee consumption during the last five years.

With the overall rate of consumption of coffee increasing at such a rapid pace, it appears to be only a matter of time before coffee overtakes tea and assumes the premier position among the non-alcoholic beverages consumed in Britain. Once this has taken place, an important aspect of the transformation of the British diet during the course of the twentieth century will have been completed, and the extent of this transformation will have come closer into focus.

The third major non-alcoholic beverage to invade the British diet during the course of the nineteenth and twentieth centuries

was cocoa. We have already seen in Chapter 3 how the rich had
been consuming drinking chocolate since its arrival in England
in the middle of the seventeenth century. The popularity of this
product was, however, limited by two major factors. In the first
place, since its introduction chocolate and the raw material used
in its production, cacao beans, were both subject to prohibitively
high duties. As early as 1660 the duty on chocolate was 8d per
gallon, and over a hundred years later, in 1776, the duty on
chocolate was 2s 3d per pound, while that on raw cacao nuts was
about 10s per hundredweight. In 1784 colonial preference was
introduced, and by 1803 the duty on non-colonial cacao had
reached a peak of 5s 10d per pound, compared with 1s 10d per
pound on cacao grown in British possessions. Thereafter the duty
began to decline, but it nevertheless remained high enough to
restrict consumption to the better-off sections of society. However,
apart from the purely financial considerations of the duty, sales
of drinking chocolate were limited by the fact that before 1828 it
was a very inferior product, very different from cocoa as we know
it today. At that time it consisted simply of ground cacao beans
mixed with sugar and sold in cake form; consequently it had a
very high butter content. This surfeit of butter had the effect of
making the drink heavy and unpalatable. In order to overcome
this problem, most chocolate manufacturers at the time resorted
to a form of adulteration, adding, among other things, starch to
absorb the butter. For example, referring in 1921 to his pre-
decessors in the firm of Cadbury Brothers around the middle of
the nineteenth century, George Cadbury declared : 'They made
a cocoa of which they were not very proud. . . . Only one-fifth
of it was cocoa, the rest being potato starch, sago, flour and
treacle. Other manufacturers made the same article—a comforting gruel.'[5]

Cocoa as we know it today had already been invented some
thirty years before the time to which George Cadbury was referring. The inventor was a Dutchman called C. J. Van Houten,
who in 1828 devised a machine for pressing out part of the butter
from the cacao bean, thus obtaining a light, more appetising and
more easily assimilated preparation than traditional drinking
chocolate. The fact that the butter which was pressed out could
be used in the manufacture of eating chocolate meant that the
new cocoa could be produced more cheaply than before, and as

the price began to fall, so the circle of consumers began to widen.

It was not until forty years after the Van Houten invention that an English firm began to produce this purer type of cocoa. The first to do so was the firm of Cadbury Brothers, who in 1866 introduced their variety called 'Cocoa Essence', upon which they built their fortunes over the next forty years. Two years later Frys followed suit, and before long the Van Houten technique was in general use in English factories. By this time the consumption of cocoa was already increasing rapidly. The turning-point had come in 1853, when Gladstone had reduced the duty on imported cacao beans to a uniform rate of 1d, at which level it remained until 1915. By 1890 the total consumption of cocoa had increased to well over 22 million lb, representing just under $\frac{2}{3}$ lb for every man, woman and child in the United Kingdom in that year. Around that time, however, a shift in demand towards a new type of cocoa, introduced by the Dutch, was already taking place. This new cocoa was flavoured with spices and treated with alkalis to intensify the taste, and it gained immediate popularity throughout the country. Rowntrees, who had been slow to adopt the Van Houten process, were the first British firm to meet this new demand when in 1887 they introduced their 'Elect' brand of cocoa. It was 1906 before Cadbury Brothers introduced 'Bournville', the brand which was to dominate the market for this new cocoa for many years after.

Consumption of cocoa continued to grow steadily during the first two decades of the twentieth century. An important factor in this growth was the development of the West African cocoa-producing area during the 1890s. Before the First World War this was already the world's leading producing area, exporting thousands of tons of cheap cocoa into Britain, which helped reduce the price of cocoa and thereby boost consumption. By 1921 the consumption per head of cocoa in Britain stood at just under 1 lb per annum. Thereafter, however, consumption of cocoa began to decline, and by 1935, despite a fall in the price from around 4s per pound in 1920 to 1s 9d in 1938, it had fallen back to under $\frac{2}{3}$ lb per head per year. After 1945 it levelled off and has remained fairly stationary ever since. In 1964 consumption per head was just over $\frac{1}{2}$ lb, and ten years later in 1973 it stood at slightly under $\frac{1}{2}$ lb. Clearly cocoa is yet another victim of rising living standards.

Apart from tea, coffee and cocoa, several other proprietary and health beverages have attained a certain degree of significance in the British diet since the latter decades of the nineteenth century. Perhaps the best-known of these is Bovril. This was the brain-child of a Scotsman, John Lawson Johnston. It was in 1873, while in Canada working to meet a contract to supply the French government with preserved beef, that Johnston first began to manufacture and sell what was then called 'Johnston's Fluid Beef'. It was a product made from meat extract which, when mixed with hot water, became a pleasant-tasting and nutritious drink. It was an immediate success, and this success continued when Johnston returned to his native Britain to set up operations in London in 1884. Within five years the demand for Bovril, as it had since become known, increased to such an extent that Johnston was unable to manage the business alone. As a result, the Bovril Company was incorporated in 1889 with a share capital of £150,000, and production increased rapidly. By the early years of the twentieth century Bovril had already become a household word throughout Britain. And in order to maintain adequate supplies of the raw material for making it, the company had extended its operations by the purchase of huge ranches and cattle herds in South America and Australia. During the First World War production reached a new peak as the company began to manufacture special ration packs for troops under government orders. The inter-war period, with all its upheavals, saw no abatement in the demand for Bovril, and the company remained highly profitable throughout the worst years of the Depression. The Second World War brought difficulties in obtaining sufficient supplies of raw materials to meet demand. Nevertheless, during the war production continued almost uninterrupted and Bovril became a valued source of variety as well as nutrition for soldiers and civilians alike. Indeed, Churchill himself was reputed to have been more than a little partial to the unlikely combination of sardines and Bovril as a bedtime snack.[6] Since 1945 the demand for Bovril, along with several other well-known branded food drinks such as Horlicks and Ovaltine, has continued to rise slightly. And despite the fact that together in 1973 they accounted for less than 4 per cent of the total expenditure on non-alcoholic beverages, they have carved an indelible mark for themselves in British dietary history.

In addition to these 'hot' drinks, Britons have been consuming a steadily increasing volume of cold drinks of various descriptions since the latter decades of the nineteenth century. The most obvious of these perhaps is milk. The average weekly consumption of this product, which stood at around 2 pints per head at the turn of the century, rose steadily, if not remarkably, during the course of the century to stand at just under 5 pints per head in 1973. This continuous rise in consumption was the result of a number of developments in the field of distribution on the one hand, and in the methods of milk production on the other. Of the former, the most important were improvements in transport facilities, particularly the introduction of motor transport during the inter-war years, the growth of several large milk wholesaling and retailing companies such as the Express Dairy Company, Cow & Gate, United Dairies (the latter two merging as Unigate Dairies in 1959) and later the Co-operative Wholesale Society and retail societies, all of whom pioneered doorstep delivery, and finally the establishment of the National Milk Marketing Board by the government in 1933 to market all milk produced on dairy farms in England and Wales. In the field of production, the most significant innovations were machine-milking, introduced towards the end of the nineteenth century following the invention of the first British continuous suction machine by William Murchland in 1889, pasteurisation and other forms of heat treatment, which spread rapidly during the inter-war years so that by 1950 over 70 per cent of all milk produced in Britain was heat-treated, and finally bottling, which was already universal by that time. Together, all these developments helped to remove the age-old problem of providing milk for the urban population of Britain in a clean and fresh state—a problem which was one of the reasons for the high rates of infant mortality which characterised Victorian Britain. In so doing, they have played a notable part in the improvement in dietary and nutritional standards which have taken place in Britain this century.

Apart from milk, which is consumed more for its food value than anything else, the twentieth century has witnessed a tremendous growth in the consumption of a wide range of soft drinks. Soft drinks are not, however, an exclusively twentieth-century discovery. Indeed, soda water was first manufactured in Britain as far back as 1790, although it was then drunk principally for medicinal purposes. During the course of the nineteenth century the popularity of carbonated water increased, flavouring followed, and the manufacture of fruit juices and non-alcoholic brewed beverages began, so that by the early years of the present century a soft drinks industry of considerable magnitude already existed in Britain. According to the Census of Production for 1907, well over 100,000 dozen bottles of table water were produced in that year, along with nearly $2\frac{1}{2}$ million gallons of fruit juices and almost a million gallons of non-alcoholic brewed beverages.

During the course of the twentieth century this industry has expanded rapidly. During the inter-war years the consumption of soft drinks more than doubled, and the output of table waters alone in 1935 was in excess of 60 million gallons. After the interruption of the Second World War, consumption continued to rise steadily. By this time a handful of large firms, including Schweppes, Tizer and Corona, were already beginning to take hold of a sizeable share of the growing national market. Brewers too were beginning to take a greater interest in soft drinks as more people began to adopt the practice of mixing spirits with various non-alcoholic drinks. In this field Schweppes became predominant and by the late fifties already accounted for three-quarters of the 'mixer' trade.

By this time, however, a huge American soft drink company had forged its way into the British market with the greatest of all soft drinks, Coca-Cola. Coca-Cola or Coke—the two are synonymous—originated in Atlanta, Georgia, in 1886. It was the invention of a pharmacist called John S. Pemberton, who originally intended it as a cure for headaches more than anything else. In the first year of its production Pemberton sold a mere twenty-five gallons of the drink. Today it is estimated that nearly 100 million bottles are consumed each day throughout the world. Coca-Cola first came to England in 1900 when Charles Howard Candler, the son of the man who had bought the Coca-Cola patent from Pemberton, brought a jug of the syrup with him on a trip to England. Since then, of course, Coca-Cola has come to dominate the British soft drinks industry, hotly pursued by its great rival Pepsi-Cola. Together they are the greatest representatives of American influence on modern British dietary habits.

Apart from these huge national firms serving mass markets and spending millions of pounds each year on advertising, the end of the Second World War brought a proliferation of small firms producing a wide range of soft drinks and serving local markets. In all, by 1960 it was estimated that there were as many as a thousand firms in the soft drinks trade, with an annual turnover in the region of £100 million. It was in that year that one of these small firms, Benjamin Shaw & Sons of Huddersfield, first introduced 'fizzy' or carbonated minerals in airtight cans under the label of 'Suncharm'. Since then, this branch of the soft drinks industry has shown the most remarkable growth; as a result, in the industry as a whole, while the number of firms had fallen to just over 500 by 1970, sales of soft drinks had doubled to nearly £200 million. In the decade up to 1973 the consumption of soft drinks rose from 63·4 pints per person per year to 100 pints. So clearly, both as accompaniments to alcoholic drinks and as refreshments in themselves, there can be no doubt that soft drinks have become an integral part of the modern British diet.

Together, tea, coffee and cocoa, along with several proprietary beverages and soft drinks, have during the last hundred years or so provided an important range of alternatives to alcohol. In their own right, however, they have become staple features of the British diet, performing a number of individual and important functions, not only as adjuncts to meals, but also as social solvents in countless types of situations. In this sense, these non-alcoholic beverages can be said to have effected a revolution of their own in British drinking habits as important, if not more so, than that characterised by the changes which have taken place in the pattern of alcohol consumption.

7

Conclusion: Future Trends in the Production and Consumption of Food

To view the development of British society since the latter decades of the nineteenth century is to look upon a process of continuous and dramatic change, punctuated and, indeed, reinforced by the upheaval caused by two world wars; to see centuries-old traditions being rudely upturned; and to see attitudes and activities become moulded by powerful economic and social forces into a characteristically modern form. In just over seventy years the industrial, occupational, geographical and demographic structures of Britain have all been transformed to such an extent that life in Britain today seems worlds apart from that which characterised the Victorian era. During the course of the twentieth century the working class, for centuries denied a say in the running of the country's life, has come to wield a mighty voice in the political arena and to demand a greater share in the wealth which it has helped to produce. Economic growth, particularly since 1945, has resulted in a great rise in living standards, so that today all but a small minority can boast that comfortable margin above subsistence which was formerly reserved for that fraction of the population who formed the middle and upper classes. As the march of technology has continued relentlessly, mechanisation has invaded almost every sphere of activity, helping to reduce the burden of heavy manual labour. An important by-product of this has been the steady decline in the length of the working week. The working man can now enjoy an amount of leisure time which his Victorian counterpart could scarcely ever have dreamed of. Women too have come to assume a new and exciting role in society. Today, for an increasing number of women childbearing and motherhood no longer represent the sole purpose in life. More and more are taking up careers in every walk of life and challenging men to deny them access to the highest positions.

In general, the twentieth century has seen a massive improvement in the quality of life for the majority of the population. This can be seen all around in dress, in housing, in education, in the possession of material goods such as cars, televisions, freezers, cookers, etc. But it is in the field of diet that the immensity of the changes which have taken place in the quality of life in Britain during the course of the twentieth century appears most vividly. This book began with a contrast : a contrast between an impoverished and underfed mass, a large proportion of whom were required to exist for much of their lives on a diet of tea, bread, margarine, condensed milk and whatever else they might be able to afford at any particular moment in time, and a society in which the demand for variety rather than sheer necessity determines what people eat; a society in which overeating and obesity rather than malnutrition is posing increasing problems. The danger of overdramatisation implicit in such a contrast cannot be ignored. 'Historical contrast', writes Peter Laslett, 'if too blankly presented may obliterate the subtler forms of change and survival.'[1] This may be true of the contrast in question, yet it serves as a valuable starting-point. It not only epitomises the magnitude of the gulf separating the Britain of today from that of just seventy years ago, but it also provides a yardstick against which the achievements of the twentieth century can be set.

The dramatic transformation which has taken place in the British diet since the latter decades of the nineteenth century must be viewed as part and parcel of the more fundamental change which has taken place in the British way of life since that time. The development of the modern diet has followed closely along the path set for it by the general movements sweeping over the economy and society of Britain. At every stage along the way, the food of the British people has been shaped to fit the emerging style of life which characterises modern Britain. Increasing affluence has led to a host of new demands in all directions. In the field of diet, the growing demand for variety has been met by the continued and extensive application of technology to the business of food production, bringing seasonal foods onto British tables all the year round and providing a wide range of new products as well as more traditional foods in more cheap and standardised forms. As leisure time has increased, so too has the popularity of labour-saving devices in the kitchen and the idea of 'convenience'.

The food industry has responded with a range of easily prepared and ready-cooked products. Since the end of the Second World War the steadily rising living standards of the majority of the population have intensified the demands being made on food producers, and the combination of the twin demands for convenience and variety has resulted in the massive growth which has occurred in the share of pre-cooked, pre-packed, ready-to-serve processed food in our diet.

The price we have had to pay for the benefits of a convenient and varied diet is nowadays measured in terms of the number of chemical additives which have become such an integral part of the business of food manufacture. Yet no one for a minute would advocate a return to the poverty diets of only seventy years ago; and the fact remains that without the use of chemical additives it would be impossible to produce a great deal of the food to which we have become so accustomed and which has become so inextricably entwined in the pattern of living today. Without it not only would our diet change, but our very way of life—a daunting prospect for even the most pioneering spirit. There can be no doubt that the benefits accruing from advances in the production and distribution of food during the present century far outweigh the drawbacks. Seventy years ago many thousands of families in Britain spent much of their lives wondering where their next meal was coming from; countless children died of malnutrition before they reached the age of one, and many of those who survived their first birthday lived only to contract horrible deficiency diseases which stunted growth and eventually crippled. Today we associate such conditions only with famine-stricken countries of the Third World and are revolted by them. The thought of such a situation existing in Britain is far removed from the minds of the majority of people. Our food has become a symbol of our economic well-being. It reflects our affluence rather than our needs. Few people today stop to ask where the food they eat has come from or what has gone into producing it. Few realise that not so long ago people could have lived comfortably on what we now dispose of as waste. The steady improvement in living standards during the twentieth century has brought for many an abundance of all the good things in life and has helped to create a state of mind in which food is taken for granted. Philosophers might argue about the morality of this, but in practical terms the achievement of this situation is an occurrence of the greatest fundamental historical significance.

But what of the future? What will we be eating in Britain twenty years from now? How much more can we afford to sacrifice in our pursuit of convenience and variety? Such questions have no easy answers. Predicting the future can be a hazardous business at the best of times, and attempts to do so in the past have left a long trail of red-faced would-be prophets. Yet if we are to plan for the future, we must have some idea of what lies ahead, and the only way to obtain this is by reference to the past. Any serious attempt to forecast the future must inevitably have some basis in a body of existing historical knowledge. Experience has shown that history is a continuum and that, barring serious upheaval, what happens in the future will invariably follow on from, and will be conditioned by, what has happened in the past. Unfortunately, as far as the economic, social and political future of Britain is concerned, the picture is complicated by Britain's entry into the European Economic Community. On the face of things, this event would appear to be of less significance than one might at first imagine, especially if account is taken of the fact that even before Britain's entry Europe was providing about 40 per cent of British imports and was taking a similar proportion of British exports. However, it is certain that as the affairs of Britain become more inextricably enmeshed in those of her European partners, the difficulty of predicting future trends in Britain in isolation will become almost insurmountable.

Nevertheless, at this stage, on the basis of a number of reasonable assumptions, it should still be possible to discern some general patterns of development which are likely to emerge in the foreseeable future. For instance, assuming that the expected economic benefits of the larger market which the EEC represents ultimately materialise, it would not be foolhardy to anticipate a level of economic growth in Britain sufficient to maintain, and possibly improve on, the gains made in the standard of living in the country since the end of the Second World War. On the basis of this, it would be no less reasonable to expect further development and consolidation of economic and social patterns which have emerged since that time. With living standards continuing to improve, it is logical to suppose that the twin demands for variety and convenience will also continue to grow. This in turn is likely to determine the course which the producers of food follow in the years to come.

However, the picture is complicated somewhat by a number of difficulties arising out of the uncertainty about future supplies and prices of food in Britain. This uncertainty stems from two sources. Firstly, and at a general level, Britain is a country which relies heavily on imports from all over the world to meet her food requirements, and therefore the availability and price of food in Britain is closely tied to movements in world commodity supplies and prices. In the past this has worked to the advantage of the British consumer, who, since the second half of the nineteenth century, has enjoyed the benefits of relatively cheap and abundant food. In recent years, however, the world food situation has changed dramatically. The spectre of overpopulation, highlighted by crop failures, drought and famine, now hangs like a cloud over the world. The relentless growth in numbers is already beginning to place an unbearable strain on the world's food resources. And there is little hope of the situation improving, with the population of the world expected to double between now and the first decade of the next century. It was estimated recently that while the demand for food in the advanced industrial countries would increase by 26 per cent between 1970 and 1985, that in developing countries would increase by some 70 per cent. This steady growth in the demand for food has already manifested itself in the form of rising food prices in industrial countries. This latter trend has been accentuated over the past three years by the soaring price of oil, which has increased the cost of fertilisers, farm machinery and food transportation. Clearly, as the world food situation deteriorates, as it most likely will, the industrial nations will have to shoulder a greater share of the burden than they have done in the past. The era of cheap food has passed for ever.

Against this background the future of British food supplies must be set. As the strain on existing sources of food intensifies, many of the foods once taken for granted in Britain, assuming they are still obtainable, are likely to soar in price. Faced with this likelihood, the British consumer could respond in a number of ways. He could pay the higher prices, if he could afford it, or he could go without. Alternatively, he could look for substitute sources of nourishment, or he could grow more of his own food. The growth of the food manufacturing industry and the increasing demand for allotments and smallholdings suggest that the latter alternatives are seen by many as the most feasible solutions to the problem of shortages and high prices of basic commodities. Indeed, the idea of national self-sufficiency in agricultural production has been mooted in many circles as the ultimate goal towards which Britain should be aiming.

In theory this idea has much to recommend itself in the current economic climate; in practice, however, it is complicated by the second, more specific, source of uncertainty about Britain's food supplies, namely her involvement, as a member country of the EEC, in the operation of the Common Agricultural Policy. How this is likely to take shape in the future and how it will affect the availability and prices of various foodstuffs in Britain, it is as yet too early to say. The common fear before Britain's entry, and one which three years' membership of the EEC has done little to dispel, was that involvement in the CAP would lead to higher food prices in Britain and hence to a decline in the standard of living in the country. This fear stemmed from the apparent differences between the long-established agricultural policy of Britain and that pursued by the EEC. For many years the British policy was centred around the idea of relatively free importation of agricultural produce from all over the world, and in particular from the Commonwealth. In conjunction with this approach, a system of direct government payments to British farmers operated. The object of this system was to make up any deficiency which might occur between market receipts and guaranteed prices for British produce, and so to assure British farmers of a reasonable return for their labour. The basis of the Common Agricultural Policy, on the other hand, is that it seeks to maintain farm incomes by the manipulation of market prices, by the use of protective tariffs and by a system of support-buying in the internal market. The dream of the architects of the policy was one of increased agricultural productivity, high and stable incomes for farmers, and stable markets which would ensure regular supplies of food at reasonable prices: undoubtedly a noble ambition. However, in practice the policy has proved more difficult to implement than originally anticipated. The paradox of the stock-piling and exporting of foodstuffs in short supply in many areas of the Community has been responsible for a great deal of mistrust of the policy-makers. The effect of the CAP on Britain so far has been, as feared by many, to raise the price of many foodstuffs in the country. Furthermore, in combination with the general trend of inflation, this increase in prices is already beginning to upset established patterns of food consumption, and if it continues indefinitely, it is bound to have serious long-term effects on the nature and composition of the British diet.

At any rate, the development of the food manufacturing industry is certain to continue, and it is equally certain that processed food will continue to account for an increasing proportion of future expenditure on food in Britain. The growing demand for variety and convenience appears at present to be almost insatiable, while rising prices for fresh agricultural produce are providing the necessary spur to the production of cheap manufactured alternatives to fresh produce. It has been estimated recently that sales of complete ready-made meals will increase by 60 per cent by 1990, while those of individual convenience foods as a whole are expected to have doubled by that time. Fortunately, developments in this area are somewhat easier to discern. Current research interests in the fields of chemistry, biochemistry, physics and engineering provide us with important clues as to the direction in which the food manufacturers see their future to lie. In a report published in 1972 by the British Food Manufacturers Industrial Research Association, the future of the food industry, as seen through the eyes of a panel of technical experts from all sections of the industry, was outlined in detail. The report, entitled *Trends in the Food Industry Over the Next Twenty Years*, drew on the results of a series of questionnaires completed by the panel of nearly forty experts. In the questionnaires the participants were required to give their opinions on a wide range of subjects relating to the future of the food industry. Among other things, they were asked to forecast future levels of food production, likely innovations, the future use of chemical additives and the likely influence of environmental and technological factors on production techniques. Under the latter heading were placed the effects of economic, social, legislative and nutritional developments. The results provide a valuable indication of how the British diet is most likely to evolve within the wider context of more general economic, social and political trends over the next twenty years or so.

For example, in terms of production, the report concluded that while the output of fresh meat and fish would increase by some 20 per cent by 1990, it also forecast that the manufacture of 'meat-like' products would increase by a similar amount. Most of us have already, either knowingly or unwittingly, sampled meat manufactured from vegetable sources. The most important vegetable used for this purpose is the soya bean. In the transmutation of the soya bean from vegetable to 'meat', the fibres of the protein extracted from it are first treated by a complicated industrial process, then spun and mixed with flour, gums and other ingredients. The result is a product almost indistinguishable to the human eye from real meat. The addition of flavouring agents and even bone and gristle completes the disguise. It has been estimated recently that in this way vegetable sources could be providing as much as 50 per cent of the protein content of our diet by 1990.[2] Indeed, it has been claimed recently that synthetic meat products are already accounting for up to 10 per cent of school meals in some local authority districts. It is clear that, with the demand for variety in diet continuing to grow, the prices of traditional foodstuffs increasing, and concern about health becoming more widespread, the soya bean might possibly provide the answer to a number of problems at the same time. On the one hand, a move towards a more vegetable-based diet would undoubtedly lower the cost of living. This arises from the fact that one acre of land planted with soya can produce between fifteen and twenty times more protein than can be produced on a similar area by traditional methods of cattle-grazing. In addition, by helping reduce our intake of fats, vegetable protein of this sort could help eliminate a serious health hazard.

In addition to the development of new products of this sort, the report also forecast a number of advances likely to occur in methods of food processing which, if applied, would have important consequences for the quality and cost of food in the future. Baking and cooking by microwave, heating by the injection of vapours, preservation by means of irradiation, mixing by the use of ultrasonics and liquid concentration by freezing were just some of the developments predicted to raise the business of food manufacture to a new peak of sophistication. In the field of packaging the report forecast the growing use of lightweight plastic containers and film with negligible permeability to air or moisture, the introduction of a non-toxic plastic pack capable of withstanding cooking temperatures, and the general use of readily disposable packaging material.

On the controversial question of the future use of chemical additives in the production of food, considerable divergence of opinion was apparent in the returns. However, a consistent upward trend in the use of natural colours and flavours and of emulsifying and stabilising agents was forecast. This was attributed in part to the predicted increase in the production of meat-like products, but also to an increase in the production of convenience foods as a whole. There was general agreement among the participants that the use of synthetic colouring would most likely be curtailed by legislative restrictions and also because of the absence of need for it. Although opinion diverged as to the future use of preservatives, it was generally anticipated that advances in methods of processing would eventually reduce the need for preserving agents. The report did, however, forecast the introduction of some new additives in the near future. The most important of these appeared to be a low-calorie sweetening agent without any other taste characteristics, enzymes and micro-organisms to develop flavour, and a new anti-oxidant which would enable the storage life of foods to be increased by fifty per cent. In general, therefore, the predictions concerning the use of additives were a mixed bunch. The key to their future would appear to lie in the attitude of future governments. Restrictive legislation would certainly have a hindering effect on the development of new products. However, in the long term, legal restrictions on the use of certain chemical additives is sure to encourage food manufacturers to develop new methods of production.

As for the organisation of the food industry itself, the report predicted that there would be a steady growth in the size of firms. It was estimated that by 1990 about 80 per cent of all food manufacturing would be in the hands of large companies. This, it was suggested, would lead to an increase in the availability of products in bulk-buying sizes. This trend is, of course, completely in line with developments taking place in the field of distribution outlined in Chapter 4. An improvement in facilities for bulk purchase would be economically extremely advantageous to the operators of superstores. In addition, such an affinity of interest between the productive and distributive sides of the food industry would almost certainly result in considerable benefits for consumers in terms of more efficient service and lower food prices. The future of the superstore and the hypermarket, of course, depends to a large extent on the cost of private motoring remaining low enough for out-of-town shopping to be economic for the individual, and on an increasing number of houses having more food storage space (and deep freezers) than at present. However, through greater integration between producers and distributors and through their sheer competitiveness, the superstore and the hypermarket should be able to maintain their cost advantage over other forms of retailer. Once planning authorities recognise the full potential of this form of shopping, it should expand rapidly to become the linchpin of the distributive system in Britain.

The future of the drink trade appears to be set on a firm course. With alcohol consumption increasing steadily, current trends on the production and sales sides of the industry are certain to be consolidated. In the near future keg beers and lager will have come to dominate the market completely, while the consumption of spirits and wine, especially the latter, is also likely to continue to grow. The transformation of the British pub, which has been as important an indication as any of the tremendous economic and social changes which have taken place in Britain during the twentieth century, will before long be completed. In *The Death of the English Pub* Christopher Hutt predicted that in the pub of the not too distant future

> The choice of wine, spirits and mineral waters will be severely restricted to the brewers' own brands. You will get the beer you are told to like, served in the fashion that the brewers want it to be served. Pub food will become more standardised and much more expensive. The décor and the furnishings will be decided by a designer in London rather than by the landlord and his wife. Entertainment in pubs will be the rule rather than the exception and you will have to take it or go dry. If you still go for a drink you will pay for the entertainment whether you want to watch it or listen to it or not.[3]

The view of a pessimist, perhaps, yet indicative of an ongoing process in the drink trade. And whatever setbacks might occur in this process through the pressure of traditionalist organisations, whatever concessions the big brewers decide to make to this section of the drinking public, they are sure to have only a marginal effect on the general trends. However, it does seem likely that the apparently choice-restrictive effects of current developments in the British pub trade will be increasingly offset by developments in other areas of the drink trade. The fact is that as the major brewers diversify their interests and break into new markets, the range of places and activities with which the consumption of alcohol will become associated is certain to expand steadily over the next twenty years or so.

To return to a more general level, the future shape of the British diet will undoubtedly be influenced to a great extent by economic and political factors. Given an upward trend in the economy over the next decade or so, the resultant rise in living standards will fuel the growing demand for variety in diet. This alone will ensure the future growth and diversification of the food and drink trades in Britain. Given also that the cost of the more traditional items in the British diet is likely to rise, the development of new products and alternative diets is likely to proceed at a rapid rate over the next few years, while increasing concern about the health value of various foods is likely to produce a move away from potentially dangerous foods. If, on the other hand, the economy fails to grow at a rate fast enough to maintain current living standards, then the diet of the British people is likely to suffer a considerable deterioration. With an increasing number of people becoming unable to afford many traditional foods, the emphasis on cheap manufactured alternatives will intensify and processed food will come to play a vital role in the diet of a large section of the population.

Whatever the economic future has in store for Britain, it is at least comforting to know that the British people are unlikely ever to see a return to the grossly deficient diets portrayed at the beginning of this book. During the course of the twentieth century our understanding of the nutritional value of foods has expanded dramatically. Science has taught us what is necessary for health, and where to obtain it. The manufacturers of food have used this knowledge to produce products which contain the nutrients necessary to maintain health and which are pleasant to the palate and the eye. Seventy years ago, without the benefit of such knowledge, the majority of the British population were condemned to a monotonous and deficient diet, which in many cases resulted in chronic illness and premature death. The gap in human knowledge which permitted that situation has thankfully been plugged for ever.

References

Where an abbreviated reference is given below, full details of the work cited will be found in the bibliography.

CHAPTER 1 (pp. 1–19)
1. T.H.S. Escott, *England: Its People, Polity and Pursuits*, London 1885, 133.
2. Jack London, *The People of the Abyss*, New York 1903, 298.
3. Georges Auguste Escoffier, *A Guide to Modern Cookery*, 2nd ed., London 1957, 785.
4. Marghanita Laski, in Nowell-Smith, ed., *Edwardian England*, 167.
5. Rowntree, *Poverty*, 275–6.
6. Robert Roberts, *The Classic Slum*, Harmondsworth 1973, 109.
7. Evidence of Dr Alfred Eicholz, H.M.I., before the Interdepartmental Committee on Physical Deterioration, 18 Dec. 1903.
8. Rowntree and Kendall, *How the Labourer Lives*, 53–8.
9. Jean-Anthelme Brillat Savarin, *La Physiologie du Gout*, Paris 1825, 1.

CHAPTER 2 (pp. 20–37)
1. Barker, McKenzie and Yudkin, ed., *Our Changing Fare*, 70.
2. Roberts, *op. cit.*, 111.
3. Quoted in *Baker and Confectioner*, 21 May 1920.
4. McCance and Widdowson, *Breads White and Brown*, 128.
5. *Ibid.*, 50.
6. Quoted in *Baker and Confectioner*, 20 Feb. 1920.
7. *Ibid.*, 5 Nov. 1926.   8. *Ibid.*, 11 Mar. 1927.
9. Cameron, *Food*, 81.
10. Quoted in *Baker and Confectioner*, 14 Dec. 1923.
11. Corley, *Quaker Enterprise*, 45.
12. See *Sunday Times*, 8 Feb. 1976.

CHAPTER 3 (pp. 38–67)
1. Evidence of J.C. Lovell before the Select Committee on the Butter Substitutes Bill, 1887.

2. Potter, *Magic Number*, 117.
3. George Orwell, *The Road to Wigan Pier* (1937), repr., Harmondsworth 1962, 179.

CHAPTER 4 (pp. 68–87)

1. Frederick Engels, *The Condition of the Working Class in England* (1892), repr., St Albans 1969, 102.
2. G.K. Chesterton, *Wine, Water and Song*, London 1915, 15–19.
3. Henry Mayhew, *London Labour and the London Poor*, Vol. I, London 1851, 158.
4. Jefferys, *Retail Trading*, 170.
5. *The Grocer*, editorial, 18 May 1895, quoted in F.G. Pennance and B.S. Yamey, 'Competition in the Retail Grocery Trade 1850–1939', *Economica*, New Series, Vol. XXII (1955), 309.
6. Cole, *Century of Co-operation*, 294.
7. See *New Society*, 4 Dec. 1975, 542.

CHAPTER 5 (pp. 88–107)

1. London, *op. cit.*, 301.
2. Rowntree and Sherwell, *Temperance Problem*, 618.
3. Carter, *Control of the Drink Trade*, 4.
4. Wilson, *Alcohol and the Nation*, 241–2.
5. Carter, *op. cit.*, 21.
6. Quoted in Arthur Marwick, *The Deluge*, London 1965, 65.
7. Carter, *op. cit.*, 158.
8. For a fuller discussion of the trend towards greater concentration in the brewing industry, see John Mark, 'The British Brewing Industry', *Lloyds Bank Review*, No. 112 (Apr. 1974).
9. *Report of the Departmental Committee on Liquor Licensing*, Cmnd. 5154, HMSO, London 1972, 65.

CHAPTER 6 (pp. 108–124)

1. Samuel Johnson, *Works*, Vol. VI, London 1825, 21.
2. Engels, *op. cit.*, 105.
3. Quoted in Wilson, *op. cit.*, 250.
4. Quoted in Wainwright, *Brooke Bond*, 39.
5. Williams, *The Firm of Cadbury*, 37.
6. Bennett, *Story of Bovril*, 27.

CHAPTER 7 (pp. 125–135)

1. Laslett, *World We Have Lost*, 247.
2. For further information on the use of soya beans, see *The Times*, 3 Apr. 1975.
3. Hutt, *Death of the English Pub*, 113–14.

Bibliography

NOTE ON STATISTICAL SOURCES

For the basic economic and social statistics, see B.R. Mitchell and Phyllis Deane, *Abstract of British Historical Statistics*, Cambridge 1962, or, alternatively, the *Annual Abstract of Statistics*, published each year by the Central Statistical Office. *Social Trends*, published annually since 1970, also by the Central Statistical Office, is another valuable source of comparative statistics. For statistics of food consumption since 1945, see the annual reports of the National Food Survey Committee entitled *Household (Domestic) Food Consumption and Expenditure*, and the *Family Expenditure Survey*, published annually since 1957 by the Department of Employment (Ministry of Labour). Pre-war statistics of consumption can be found in Richard Stone et al., *The Measurement of Consumers' Expenditure and Behaviour in the United Kingdom 1920–1938*, Cambridge 1953, and in A.R. Prest (assisted by A.A. Adams), *Consumers' Expenditure in the United Kingdom 1900–1919*, Cambridge 1954. Detailed statistics of production of various foodstuffs can be found in the government Censuses of Production, which date back to 1907.

I. GENERAL WORKS ON ECONOMIC, SOCIAL AND DIETARY HISTORY

Abrams, Mark Alexander, *The Condition of the British People 1911–1945*, London 1945

Ashworth, William, *An Economic History of England 1870–1939*, London 1960

Barker, T.C., McKenzie, J.C. and Yudkin, John, ed., *Our Changing Fare: Two Hundred Years of British Food Habits*, London 1966

Beveridge, Sir William, *British Food Control*, London 1928

Booth, Charles, *Life and Labour of the People in London* (1889–91), repr., London 1902

Burnett, John, *Plenty and Want: A Social History of Diet in England from 1815 to the Present Day*, London 1966

Burnett, John, *A History of the Cost of Living*, Harmondsworth 1969

Cameron, Allan G., *Food—Facts and Fallacies*, London 1971

Cecil, Robert, *Life in Edwardian England*, London 1969

Cole, G.D.H. and Postgate, Raymond, *The Common People 1746–1946*, 2nd ed. (revised and partly rewritten), London 1946

Crawford, Sir William and Broadley, H., *The People's Food*, London 1938

Curtis-Bennett, Sir Noel, *The Food of the People, Being the History of Industrial Feeding*, London 1949

Drummond, J.C. and Wilbraham, Anne, *The Englishman's Food: A History of Five Centuries of English Diet* (1939), 2nd ed., revised, with a new chapter by Dorothy Hollingsworth, London 1957

Graves, Robert and Hodge, Alan, *The Long Weekend: A Social History of Great Britain 1918–1939* (1940), repr., Harmondsworth 1971

Halsey, A.H., *Trends in British Society Since 1900*, London 1972

Laslett, Peter, *The World We Have Lost*, London 1965

Marsh, David C., *The Changing Social Structure of England and Wales 1871–1961*, revised ed., London 1965

Marwick, Arthur, *The Explosion of British Society 1914–1970*, London 1971

Marwick, Arthur, *Britain in the Century of Total War: War, Peace and Social Change 1900–1967*, repr., Harmondsworth 1970

Nowell-Smith, S., ed., *Edwardian England 1901–1914*, London 1964

Oddy, D.J. and Miller, D.S., ed., *The Making of the Modern British Diet*, London 1976

Orr, John Boyd, *Food, Health and Income. Report on a Survey of Adequacy of Diet in Relation to Income*, London 1936

Pollard, Sydney, *The Development of the British Economy 1914–1967*, London 1969

Rowntree, B. Seebohm, *Poverty: A Study in Town Life*, London 1901

Rowntree, B. Seebohm and Kendall, May, *How the Labourer Lives: A Study of the Rural Labour Problem*, London 1913

Smith, Charles, *Britain's Food Supplies in Peace and War*, London 1940

Tannahill, Reay, *Food in History*, London 1973

Yudkin, J. and McKenzie, J.C., *Changing Food Habits*, London 1964

2. WORKS ON SPECIFIC SUBJECTS

Accum, Frederick, *A Treatise on Adulterations of Food and Culinary Poisons*, London 1820

Ashley, Sir William, *The Bread of Our Forefathers: An Inquiry in Economic History*, Oxford 1928

Baker, Stanley, *Milk to Market: Forty Years of Milk Marketing*, London 1973

Bellamy, J., *British Markets for Flour and Wheatfeed*, Hull 1957

Bennett, Richard, *The Story of Bovril*, London 1953

Bitting, A.W., *Appertizing: or, the Art of Canning: Its History and Development*, San Francisco 1937

Cadbury Brothers Ltd, *Industrial Record 1919–1939: A Review of the Inter-War Years*, London 1941

Cadbury Brothers Ltd, *Industrial Challenge: The Experience of Cadburys of Bournville in the Post-War Years*, London 1964

Carr-Saunders, A.M., Sargant, Florence P., Peers, R. et al., *Consumers' Co-operation in Great Britain: An Examination of the British Co-operative Movement*, London 1938

Carter, Henry, *The Control of the Drink Trade: A Contribution to National Efficiency during the Great War 1915–1918*, London 1919

Cole, G.D.H., *A Century of Co-operation*, Manchester 1944

Corley, T.A.B., *Quaker Enterprise in Biscuits: Huntley and Palmers of Reading 1822–1972*, London 1972

Davis, Dorothy, *A History of Shopping*, London 1966

Dietz, Lawrence, *Soda Pop: The History, Advertising, Art and Memorabilia of Soft Drinks in America*, New York 1973

Forrest, D.M., *Tea for the British: The Social and Economic History of a Famous Trade*, London 1973

Forrest, D.M., *A Hundred Years of Ceylon Tea 1867–1967*, London 1967

General Foods Ltd, *The Food Makers: A History of General Foods Ltd*, Banbury 1972

Griffiths, Sir Percival, *The History of the Indian Tea Industry*, London 1967

Heer, Jean, *World Events 1866–1966: The First Hundred Years of Nestlé*, Lausanne 1966

Hovis Ltd, *The Hovis Jubilee: A Brief Record of the Company's History between 1898–1948*, London 1948

Hurst, A.H., *The Bread of Britain*, London 1930

Hutt, Christopher, *The Death of the English Pub*, London 1973

Janes, Hurford, *The Red Barrel: A History of Watney Mann*, London 1963

Jefferys, James Bavington, *Retail Trading in Britain 1850–1950: A Study of Trends in Retailing with Special Reference to the Development of Co-operative, Multiple Shop and Department Store Methods of Trading*, Cambridge 1954

Jefferys, James Bavington, *The Distribution of Consumer Goods*, Cambridge 1950

Jenkins, Alan, *Drinka Pinta: The Story of Milk and the Industry that Serves It*, London 1970

Jones, Osman and Jones, T.W., *Canning Production and Control*, 3rd ed., London 1941

Kahn, E.J. jr, *The Big Drink: An Unofficial History of Coca-Cola*, London 1960

Knapp, A.W., *The Cocoa and Chocolate Industry*, 2nd ed., London 1930

Kuipers, J.D., *Resale Price Maintenance in Great Britain: With Special Reference to the Grocery Trade*, Wageningen 1950

McCance, R.A. and Widdowson, E.M., *Breads White and Brown: Their Place in Thought and Social History*, London 1956

MacGregor, D.R., *The Tea Clippers: An Account of the China Tea Trade and Some of the British Sailing Ships Engaged in It from 1849 to 1869*, London 1972

Mathias, Peter, *The Brewing Industry in England 1700–1830*, Cambridge 1959

Mathias, Peter, *Retailing Revolution: A History of Multiple Retailing in the Food Trades based upon the Allied Suppliers Group of Companies*, London 1967

Maunder, P., *The Bread Industry in the United Kingdom*, Nottingham 1970

Morgan, Bryan, *Express Journey 1864–1964: A Centenary History of the Express Dairy Company Limited*, London 1964

National Economic Development Office, *The Future Pattern of Shopping* (A report prepared by NEDO for the Distributive Trades Economic Development Committee), London 1971

Potter, Stephen, *The Magic Number: The Story of '57'*, London 1959

Pudney, John, *A Draught of Contentment: The Story of the Courage Group*, London 1971

Reader, W.J., *Birds Eye: The Early Years*, Walton-on-Thames 1963

Redfern, Percy, *The New History of the C.W.S.*, London 1938

Rowntree, Joseph and Sherwell, Arthur, *The Temperance Problem and Social Reform*, 7th ed., London 1900

Rubinstein, Stanley, *The Street Trader's Lot, London 1851: Being an Account of the Lives, Miseries, Joys and Chequered Activi-*

ties of London Street Sellers as Recorded by their Contemporary Henry Mayhew, London 1947

Sheppard, R. and Newton, E. *The Story of Bread*, London 1957

Strong, L.A.G., *A Brewer's Progress 1757–1957: A Survey of Charrington's Brewery on the Occasion of its Bicentenary*, London 1957

Vaizey, John, *The Brewing Industry 1886–1951: An Economic Study*, London 1960

Vernon, Anne, *A Quaker Businessman: The Life of Joseph Rowntree 1836–1925*, London 1958

Wainwright, David, *Brooke Bond: A Hundred Years*, London 1969

Waugh, Alec, *The Lipton Story: A Centennial Biography*, London 1951

Williams, Iola, *The Firm of Cadbury 1831–1931*, London 1931

Wilson, Charles, *The History of Unilever: A Study in Economic Growth and Social Change*, 2 vols, London 1954

Wilson, George B., *Alcohol and the Nation: A Contribution to the Study of the Liquor Problem in the United Kingdom from 1800 to 1935*, London 1940

Woodcock, F.H. and Lewis, W.R., *Canned Foods and the Canning Industry*, London 1938

Index